DAILY JAPANESE
Words & Phrases

Written by Michiko Kasahara
English edited by Pamela Fields

GOKEN

Preface

Everyday many people visit Japan. However, there are not many English-speaking employees in big hotels, travel agencies, and department stores. Therefore this useful book is designed to help you enjoy your stay more in Japan.

I hope that you will challenge your Japanese skills and try to communicate with Japanese people. If you bring this book with you, it may help bridge the language gap.

It contains many useful and polite expressions pertinent to Japanese language, life, and customs. If you can't express in Japanese what you want to say, simply find the page that contains the English equivalent, and pronounce the romanized Japanese expression or show it to the person you're addressing.

This book will make your stay more ·comfortable and rewarding. It will enable you to widen the range

of your activities and make good Japanese friends.

I hope you will enjoy your stay in Japan.

November 1988

Michiko Kasahara

CONTENTS

How to use this book

This book contains various expressions and words. Please choose the expressions or words you need depending on the situation. The words combined with hyphens are pronounced as one unit.

left side	right side
How are you? (English)	Ogenki desu- ka. (Romanized Japanese)

★ A word in parenthes (　) can be omitted.
★ A word in brackets [　] can be substituted for the word preceding it.

Hiragana and Katakana

We use the modified Hepburn system.

roomaji	hiragana	(katakana)

Vowels

a あ(ア)	i い(イ)	u う(ウ)	e え(エ)	o お(オ)

Consonant plus vowel sound

ka か(カ)	ki き(キ)	ku く(ク)	ke け(ケ)	ko こ(コ)
sa さ(サ)	shi し(シ)	su す(ス)	se せ(セ)	so そ(ソ)
ta た(タ)	chi ち(チ)	tsu つ(ツ)	te て(テ)	to と(ト)
na な(ナ)	ni に(ニ)	nu ぬ(ヌ)	ne ね(ネ)	no の(ノ)
ha は(ハ)	hi ひ(ヒ)	fu ふ(フ)	he へ(ヘ)	ho ほ(ホ)
ma ま(マ)	mi み(ミ)	mu む(ム)	me め(メ)	mo も(モ)
ya や(ヤ)		yu ゆ(ユ)		yo よ(ヨ)
ra ら(ラ)	ri り(リ)	ru る(ル)	re れ(レ)	ro ろ(ロ)
wa わ(ワ)				o* を(ヲ)

ga が(ガ)	gi ぎ(ギ)	gu ぐ(グ)	ge げ(ゲ)	go ご(ゴ)
za ざ(ザ)	ji じ(ジ)	zu ず(ズ)	ze ぜ(ゼ)	zo ぞ(ゾ)
da だ(ダ)	ji** ぢ(ヂ)	zu*** づ(ヅ)	de で(デ)	do ど(ド)
ba ば(バ)	bi び(ビ)	bu ぶ(ブ)	be べ(ベ)	bo ボ(ボ)
pa ぱ(パ)	pi ぴ(ピ)	pu ぷ(プ)	pe ぺ(ペ)	po ぽ(ポ)

Sounds with -ya,-yu, and -yo

kya	きゃ(キャ)	kyu	きゅ(キュ)	kyo	きょ(キョ)
sha	しゃ(シャ)	shu	しゅ(シュ)	sho	しょ(ショ)
cha	ちゃ(チャ)	chu	ちゅ(チュ)	cho	ちょ(チョ)
nya	にゃ(ニャ)	nyu	にゅ(ニュ)	nyo	にょ(ニョ)
hya	ひゃ(ヒャ)	hyu	ひゅ(ヒュ)	hyo	ひょ(ヒュ)
mya	みゃ(ミャ)	myu	みゅ(ミュ)	myo	みょ(ミョ)
rya	りゃ(リャ)	ryu	りゅ(リュ)	ryo	りょ(リョ)
gya	ぎゃ(ギャ)	gyu	ぎゅ(ギュ)	gyo	ぎょ(ギョ)
ja	じゃ(ジャ)	ju	じゅ(ジュ)	jo	じょ(ジョ)
bya	びゃ(ビャ)	byu	びゅ(ビュ)	byo	びょ(ビョ)
pya	ぴゃ(ピャ)	pyu	ぴゅ(ピュ)	pyo	ぴょ(ピョ)

8

*   This "を" is used to show the particle "o".

**   The "ji" sound is usually written with "じ".

***   The "zu" sound is usually written with "ず".

Syllabic consonant

| n ん(ン) | This sound is represented by "n" in the romanization used in this book. We use

"shinbun" instead of "shimbun".

"n" is the only independent consonant not combined with a vowel.

kin'en	ki-n-en	no smoking
kinen	ki-ne-n	anniversary

Before "m", "p", "b", it is pronounced "m".

  Ex. enpitsu (pencil)

Before "n", "t", "d", "z", it is pronounced "n".

  Ex. ningen (man)

Before "k", "g", "ng", it is pronounced "ng".

  Ex. kongetsu (this month)

Double consonants

p, t, s, k tsu っ（ッ）			
pp	tt	ss	kk
kippu きっぷ	kitte きって	issai いっさい	gakkoo がっこう
ch→tch	ts→tts	sh→ssh	
matchi マッチ	yottsu よっつ	zasshi ざっし	

Long vowels

The use of hiragana for two successive vowels.

aa(ā)	ああ （アー）	Ex.	okaasan おかあさん	mother
ii(ī)	いい （イー）		tanoshii たのしい	happy
uu(ū)	うう （ウー）		yuubin ゆうびん	mail
ee(ē) ei	ええ，えい（エー）		gakusee がくせい	student
oo(ō) ou	おお，おう（オー）		otooto おとうと	brother

We use "yuubin" instead of "yūbin".

Three kinds of Japanese writing

Kanji	Chinese characters or ideographs
Hiragana	phonetic syllabary
Katakana	phonetic syllabary

Foreign names and foreign loan words are written in katakana.

The use of hiragana for particles

は(wa)	Watashi - **wa** sensee desu.
	わたし　は せんせい です。
	I am　　a　　teacher.
へ(e)	Ginza - **e** ikitai-desu.
	ぎんざ へ　いきたいです。
	I want to go to Ginza.
を(o)	Kippu - **o** kaimasu.
	きっぷ を　かいます。
	I buy a ticket.

Accent

Japanese	pitch accent	Ex. k̄āki oyster kak̄ī persimmon
English	stress accent	ɔ́istər oyster pərsímən persimmon

┌─────────── **Cassette tapes available** ───────────┐

The phrases in this book are recorded on two cassette tapes. Because the recording has been done in stereo, you can hear the English only on the left channel, and Japanese only on the right channel. Therefore, if you adjust the balance on your cassette recorder so that you can hear only the English, you can practice saying the Japanese equivalent and then check your response.

Of course, you can listen to the recording on a machine whose balance can't be adjusted.

└──┘

I

Essential
Words and Phrases

Greetings (1)

1. Hello.	Konnichiwa.
2. Good morning.	Ohayoo-gozaimasu.
3. Good afternoon.	Konnichiwa.
4. Good evening.	Konbanwa.
5. Good night.	Oyasuminasai.
6. Good bye.	Sayoonara.
7. See you later.	Dewa mata./Mata atode.
8. See you tomorrow.	Mata ashita.
9. How do you do?	Hajimemashite.
10. Nice to meet you.	Doozo yoroshiku.
11. I'm glad to see you.	Oaideki-te ureshii-desu.

Greetings (2)

1. How are you?	Ogenki desu-ka.
2. I'm fine, thank you.	Arigatoo. Genki-desu.
And you?	Anata-wa.
3. I'm fine, too.	Watashi-mo genki-desu.
Thank you.	Arigatoo-gozaimasu.

Farewell (1)

1. I must go soon.　　　Sorosoro ikanakereba-
　　　　　　　　　　　narimasen.

2. Please come again.　Zehi mata okoshi-
　　　　　　　　　　　kudasai.

Farewell (2)

1. I hope I'll see you　Mata oai-shimashoo.
   again.

2. When shall we meet　Kondo-wa itsu oai-
   again?　　　　　　　dekimasu-ka.

3. I'll see you on Mon-　Getsuyoobi-ni oai-
   day.　　　　　　　　shimashoo.

4. I'll see you soon.　　Chikajika mata aimashoo.

5. I'd like to come　　Mata kitai-desu.
   again.

Farewell (3)

1. Please give my best　Tanaka-san-ni yoroshiku
   regards to Mr. Tana-　otsutae-kudasai.

ka.

2. Please give my regards to everyone.   Minasama-ni yoroshiku.

Farewell (4)

1. Take care.   Ki-o tsukete.
2. Please don't work too hard.   Amari muri-o shinaide-kudasai.

Miscellaneous formalities

1. I'm looking forward to your letter.   Otegami tanoshimi-ni shite-imasu.
2. Congratulations.   Omedetoo-gozaimasu.

Expressions of thanks (1)

1. Thank you very much.   Doomo arigatoo-gazaimasu.
2. Thank you.   Arigatoo-gozaimasu.
3. Thanks a lot.   Doomo arigatoo.
4. Thanks.   Arigatoo./Doomo.

Replies

1. You're welcome./   Doo itashimashite.
   Not at all.   / Don't
   mention it.

2. The pleasure is   Kochira koso.
   mine.

Expressions of thanks (2)

1. Thank you very   Iroiro-to osewa-ni nari
   much for everything.   arigatoo-gozaimashita.

2. It's very kind of   Goshinsetsu arigatoo-
   you.   gozaimasu.

3. Thank you for your   Otesuu-o
   trouble.   okakeshimashita.

Preceding expressions of thanks

1. It was a lot of fun.   Totemo
   tanoshikatta-desu.

2. I've enjoyed talking   Ohanashi-dekite
   to you.   tanoshikatta-desu.

Expressions of apology (1)

1. I'm sorry./Excuse me./Sorry.	Sumimasen[Suimasen]./ Gomennasai./ Mooshiwake-arimasen./ Shitsuree shimasu.
2. I'm really sorry.	Hontoo-ni mooshiwake-arimasen.

Expressions of apology (2)

1. I'm sorry to have troubled you.	Gomendoo-o okakeshite mooshiwake-arimasen.
2. I'm sorry to have kept you waiting.	Omataseshite sumimasen.

Replies

1. Don't worry about it./That's OK.	Goshinpai naku.
2. Never mind.	Doozo ki-ni nasarazuni./ Doozo shinpai-shinaide.
3. You're welcome. (=	Doo itashimashite.

Never mind.)／

That's all right.

Approaching a person

1. Excuse me.   Sumimasen.

2. Sir !／Miss !／   Sumimasen.
   Madam !

3. Mr. ∼./Mrs. ∼./   ∼ san.
   Ms. ∼./Miss ∼.

4. Hello.   Konnichiwa.

Entering someone's room

1. Hello, I hope I'm   Konnichiwa.
   not disturbing you.   Ojamashimasu.

2. Excuse me, I'll   Shitsuree-shimasu.
   come in.   (Hairi-masu.)

Welcoming someone to your home

1. Please come in.   Doozo ohairi-kudasai.

2. Please come in［step   Doozo oagari-kudasai.

up].

3. Please make your-   Doozo oraku-ni.
   self at home.

Affirmative replies

1. Yes.   Hai.
2. I got it./I see./I   Wakarimashita.
   understand./Certain-
   ly.
3. I know.   Wakatte-imasu.
4. Yes, that's true.   Soo desu-ne.
5. Yes, I think so.   Hai, soo omoimasu.
6. That's right.   Sono toori-desu.
7. I'm all right./It's all   Daijoobu desu.
   right.
8. That'll be all right.   Sore-de kekko-desu.
9. Yes, quite true.   Hai, mattaku sono
                             tooridesu.
10. I'm sure.   Tashika desu.
11. I hope so.   Sooda-to ii-desu-ne.

12. That sounds inter-   Omoshiro-soo desu-ne.
    esting.

13. My pleasure.   Yorokonde.

Negative replies

1. No.   Iie.

2. I don't know.   Wakarimasen.

3. I'm not sure.   Hakkiri wakarimasen.

4. I don't think so.   Soo-wa omoimasen.

5. I didn't know that.   Sore-wa shirimasen-
                          deshita.

6. I don't remember.   Oboete-imasen.

7. I don't remember   Yoku oboete-imasen.
   clearly.

8. That's too bad.   Sore-wa taihen-desu-
                          ne./Sore-wa okinodoku-
                          desu-ne.

9. It's impossible.   Sore-wa muri-desu.

10. Don't get   me   Gokai-shinai-de kudasai.
    wrong.

Exclamatory replies

1. That's great!   Sugoi-desu-ne.

                          (Ii-desu-ne.)

2. That sounds good.   Ii-desu-ne.

3. That'll be fine.   Sore-wa kekko-desu-ne.

Miscellaneous

1. Are you sure?   Tashika-desu-ka.

2. Let me see.   Eeto.

Forms of "I don't understand."

1. Pardon?／Sorry?   Nan desu-ka.

2. I don't understand.   Wakarimasen.

3. I'm sorry, I didn't   Gomennasai, kikitore-
   get that.   masen-deshita.

Forms of "Please speak more slowly."

1. Could you speak   Motto yukkuri
   more slowly?   hanashite-itadakemasu-
                          ka.

2. Could you repeat it more slowly ?

Motto yukkuri kurikaeshite-kudasai.

Forms of "Please repeat that."

1. Once again, please.

Moo ichido onegai-shimasu.

2. Will you tell me again, please ?

Moo ichido itte-itadake-masu-ka.

3. Could you please say that again in simpler language ?

Motto yasashii kotoba-de moo ichido itte-kudasai.

4. Please say it in English.

Eego-de onegai-shimasu.

5. What did he say ?

Kare-wa nan-to iimashita-ka.

Forms of "I don't speak Japanese well."

1. I can't speak well.

Joozu-ni hanasukoto-ga dekimasen.

2. I can't find the

Tekitoo-na kotoba-ga

proper words.	mitsukarimasen.
3. Can you understand my Japanese ?	Watashi-no nihongo-ga wakarimasu-ka.
4. I didn't mean that.	Sonna tsumori-de itta-no-dewa arimasen.
5. He doesn't understand Japanese at all.	Kare-wa mattaku nihongo-ga wakarimasen.

Forms of "What do you mean ?"

1. What does it mean ?	Dooyuu imi desu-ka.
2. What do you mean ?	Dooyuu imi deshoo-ka.

Requests (1)

1. May I ask a favor of you ?	Onegai-shite-mo yoroshii-desu-ka.
2. May I interrupt you for a moment ?	Chotto ojama-shite-mo yoroshii-desu-ka.
3. Could you help me ?	Tetsudatte-itadakemasu-ka.

4. Please.   Onegai-shimasu.

5. ～, please.   ～- o onegai-shimasu.

6. Please give me ～.   ～-o kudasai.

7. If you don't mind,   Moshi gomeiwaku-de
   ....   nakereba....

Requests (2)

1. Could you write it   Koko-ni kaite-itadake
   down here?   masu-ka.

2. Please write.   Tegami-o kudasai.

Forms of "Please hurry."

1. Please hurry.   Isoide-itadake-masu-ka.

2. It's an emergency.   Kinkyuu-nano-desu.

Forms of "Wait, please."

1. Just a minute.   Chotto matte-kudasai.

2. Just a moment,   Shooshoo omachi
   please.   kudasai.

3. Will you please   Shibaraku matte-

wait?	itadake-masu-ka.
4. Could you wait for a few more minutes?	Moo ni-san-pun matte-kudasai-masu-ka.
5. I'll be thirty minutes late.	Sanjuppun osoku narimasu.

Forms of "No, thank you."

1. No, thank you.	Iie kekko-desu.
2. I don't need it, thank you.	(Sore-wa) Hitsuyoo-arimasen. Doomo arigatoo.
3. I don't like it.	Amari suki-dewa arimasen.
4. I don't want to do it.	Ki-ga susumimasen.
5. I'm sorry, but I can't do it.	Zannen-desu-ga, dekimasen.

Asking for permission

1. Is this all right?	Kore-de ii-desu-ka.

2. May I take a picture? — Shashin-o totte-mo ii-desu-ka.

3. May I smoke? — Tabako-o sutte-mo ii-desu-ka.

Self introduction

1. I'm not Japanese. — Watashi-wa gaikokujin desu.

2. I'm not familiar with this area. — Konoatari-wa yoku shirimasen.

3. We can't speak Japanese. — Watashitachi-wa nihongo-ga hanasemasen.

4. What country are you from? — Okuni-wa dochira desu-ka.

5. I'm from Korea. — Kankoku desu.

6. I'm from New York. — Nyuuyooku-no shusshin desu.

7. Why did you come to Japan? — Dooshite Nihon-ni kita-no-desu-ka.

8. To attend a meeting in Tokyo.

Tookyoo-no kaigi-ni shusseki-suru-tame-desu.

9. I've come here to study.

Benkyoo-suru-tame-ni kimashita.

10. I'm traveling.

Ryokoochuu desu.

11. What are you doing in Japan?

Anata-wa nihon-de nani-o shiteiru-no-desu-ka.

12. I'm studying Japanese art.

Nihon-no bijutsu-o manande-imasu.

13. How long have you been in Japan?

Anata-wa dono-kurai Nihon-ni sunde-imasu-ka.

14. (I have been in Japan) for two years.

Ninen desu.

15. What kind of work do you do?

Oshigoto-wa nan desu-ka.

16. I work for a publishing company.

Shuppansha-de hataraite-imasu.

17. Is a Japanese interpreter available? Nihonjin-no tsuuyaku-o onegai-dekimasu-ka.

18. Do you have any identification? Mibun-o shoomee-suru-mono-o nani-ka motte-imasu-ka.

Questions for conversing

1. May I have your name, please? Onamae-o oshiete-itadake-masu-ka.

2. My name is ∼. Watashi-no namae-wa ∼ desu.

3. Where do you live? Doko-ni sunde-imasu-ka.

4. I live in ∼. ∼-ni sunde imasu.

5. How about you? Anata-wa ikaga desu-ka.

6. I agree with your opinion. Watashi-mo anata-no iken-ni sansee desu.

7. Any trouble? Nani-ka komattakoto-ga aru-no-desu-ka.

8. Do you like it? Osuki desu-ka.

9. Do you like it ?   Kiniirimashita-ka.

Asking for an explanation

1. What's happened ?   Nani-ga atta-no-desu-ka.

2. What should I do ?   Doo-sureba ii-deshoo-ka.

3. Please tell me the reason.   Riyuu-o oshiete-kudasai.

4. Why ?   Naze-desu-ka./ Dooshite-desu-ka.

5. Because....   Nazenara....

6. What is the reason ?   Gen'in-wa nan-desu-ka.

7. What's it for ?   Nan-no tame desu-ka.

8. Please explain this in detail.   Kuwashiku setsumee-shite-kudasai.

9. What does the sign say ?   Ano sain-wa nan-desu-ka.

10. How do you read this ?   Kono-ji-wa doo yomimasu-ka.

11. What's the meaning of this word?   Kono kotoba-no imi-wa nan desu-ka.

12. What does this character mean?   Kono-ji-wa dooyuu imi desu-ka.

13. How do you say this in Japanese?   Kore-o nihongo-de nan-to iimasu-ka.

Asking for dates and time

1. What time is it now?   Nan-ji desu-ka.

2. Do you have the time?   Ima, nan-ji-ka wakari-masu-ka.

3. What day of the week is it?   Kyoo-wa nan-yoobi desu-ka.

4. What's the date?   Kyoo-wa nan-nichi desu-ka.

Asking about places

1. Where is it?   Basho-wa doko desu-ka.

2. Where am I?   Koko-wa doko desu-ka.

3. Where's the toilet?   Toire-wa doko desu-ka.

Miscellaneous (1)

1. How's the weather today?   Kyoo-no tenki-wa doo desu-ka.

2. How much is it?   Ikura desu-ka.

3. Who is he [she]?   Ano hito-wa dare desu-ka.

4. Please tell me who he [she] is.   Ano kata-wa donata desu-ka. (*Polite style*)

Miscellaneous (2)

1. Here you are.   Hai, kore desu.

2. Go ahead, please.   Doozo.

3. After you, please,   Doozo, osaki-ni.

4. Later, please.   Ato-de onegai-shimasu.

5. It depends on ∼.   ∼-ni yorimasu.

6. It depends on the circumstances.   Toki-to-baai-ni yorimasu.

Pronouns

I	watashi
we	watakushitachi
you	anata
you (*pl.*)	anatatachi
she	kanojo
he	kare
they	karera/kanojora/sorera
this	kore/kono
that	are, sore/ano, sono
it	sore
my	watashi-no
your	anata-no
his	kare-no
her	kanojo-no
its	sore-no, are-no, sono
their	karera-no/kanojora-no/
	sorera-no

Family

(your) father	otoosan
(my) father	chichi

(your) mother	okaasan
(my) mother	haha
(your) (older) brother	oniisan
(my) (older) brother	ani
(your) (younger) brother	otootosan
(my) (younger) brother	otooto
(your) (older) sister	oneesan
(my) (older) sister	ane
(your) (younger) sister	imootosan
(my) (younger) sister	imooto
(your) uncle	ojisan
(my) uncle	oji
(your) aunt	obasan
(my) aunt	oba
(your) grandfather	ojiisan

(my) grandfather	sofu
(your) grand-mother	obaasan
(my) grandmother	sobo
(your) wife	okusan
(my) wife	kanai, tsuma
(your) husband	goshujin
(my) husband	shujin
(your) son	musukosan
(my) son	musuko
(your) daughter	musumesan
(my) daughter	musume .
(your) child, (your) children	kodomosan/okosan
(my) child	kodomo
(my) children	kodomotachi

Adjectives

good, fine, right	ii, yoi
bad	warui
slow (↔fast), late (↔early)	osoi

fast, early, speedy, quick, swift	hayai
happy	ureshii
pleasant	tanoshii
interesting	omoshiroi
of little importance, boring, uninteresting	tsumaranai
cute, charming, pretty	kawaii
beautiful	utsukushii
nice, great	suteki, kirei
sweet	amai
salty	shiokarai
hot (*Ex.* curry, spice)	karai
delicious	oishii
wide, large, open	hiroi
narrow, tight small	semai
light (*weight*)	karui
heavy (*weight*)	omoi

thin, slender	hosoi
thick, fat	futoi
heavy, thick	atsui
thin, light	usui
loose	yurui
tight	kitsui
long	nagai
short	mijikai
round	marui
square	shikakui
light (*color*), bright	akarui (*iro*)
horrible, frightening	kowai
soft, mild	yawarakai
hard, tight, firm	katai
dark	kurai
detailed	kuwashii
warm	atatakai
cool	suzushii
hot	atsui
cold	samui

weak	yowai
strong	tsuyoi
easy, simple, plain, gentle	yasashii
high	takai
low	hikui
far	tooi
near	chikai
cheap	yasui
expensive	takai
small, little	chiisai
large, big	ookii

Adverbs

well	joozuni, umaku, yoku
badly	hetani, waruku

Cardinal numbers

0	zero
1	ichi
2	ni
3	san

4	shi, yon
5	go
6	roku
7	shichi, nana
8	hachi
9	kyuu, ku
10	juu
11	juu-ichi
12	juu-ni
13	juu-san
14	juu-shi, juu-yon
15	juu-go
16	juu-roku
17	juu-shichi
18	juu-hachi
19	juu-ku, juu-kyuu
20	nijuu
21	nijuu-ichi
22	nijuu-ni
23	nijuu-san
24	nijuu-shi
25	nijuu-go

26	nijuu-roku
27	nijuu-shichi
28	nijuu-hachi
29	nijuu-ku
30	sanjuu
31	sanjuu-ichi
32	sanjuu-ni
33	sanjuu-san
40	yonjuu
41	yonjuu-ichi
42	yonjuu-ni
43	yonjuu-san
44	yonjuu-yon
50	gojuu
60	rokujuu
70	shichijuu, nanajuu
80	hachijuu
90	kyuujuu
100	hyaku
101	hyaku-ichi
111	hyaku-juuichi
120	hyaku-nijuu

130	hyaku-sanjuu
140	hyaku-yonjuu
150	hyaku-gojuu
160	hyaku-rokujuu
170	hyaku-nanajuu
180	hyaku-hachijuu
190	hyaku-kyuujuu
200	nihyaku
300	sanbyaku
400	yonhyaku
500	gohyaku
600	roppyaku
700	nanahyaku
800	happyaku
900	kyuuhyaku
1,000	sen
1,500	sen-gohyaku
2,000	nisen
3,000	sanzen
4,000	yonsen
5,000	gosen
6,000	rokusen

7,000	nanasen
8,000	hassen
9,000	kyuusen
10,000	ichiman
20,000	niman
30,000	sanman
40,000	yonman
50,000	goman
60,000	rokuman
70,000	nanaman
80,000	hachiman
90,000	kyuuman
100,000	juuman
1000,000	hyakuman
10,000,000	issenman

Time

time	jikan, toki, jikoku
~ o'clock	~ ji
1 o'clock	ichiji
2 o'clock	niji
3 o'clock	sanji

4 o'clock	yoji
5 o'clock	goji
6 o'clock	rokuji
7 o'clock	shichiji
8 o'clock	hachiji
9 o'clock	kuji
10 o'clock	juuji
11 o'clock	juuichiji
12 o'clock	juuniji
～ minute(s)	～ fun, ～ pun
1 minute	ippun
2 minutes	nifun
3 minutes	sanpun
4 minutes	yonpun
5 minutes	gofun
6 minutes	roppun
7 minutes	nanafun
8 minutes	happun, hachifun
9 minutes	kyuufun
10 minutes	jippun, juppun
11 minutes	juuippun
12 minutes	juunifun

20 minutes	nijippun, nijuppun
30 minutes	sanjippun, sanjuppun, han
40 minutes	yonjippun, yonjuppun
50 minutes	gojippun, gojuppun
55 minutes	gojuugofun
~ second(s)	~ byoo
1 second	ichibyoo
10 seconds	juubyoo
35 seconds	sanjuugo byoo
~ hour(s)	~ jikan
1 hour	ichijikan
2 hours	nijikan
3 hours	sanjikan
4 hours	yojikan
5 hours	gojikan
6 hours	rokujikan
7 hours	shichijikan
8 hours	hachijikan
9 hours	kujikan
10 hours	juujikan

Other time words

now	ima
after	ato
later	atode
before	mae
today	kyoo
yesterday	kinoo
the day before yes-terday	ototoi
tomorrow	ashita
the day after tomorrow	asatte
this week	konshuu
last week	senshuu
the week before last	sensenshuu
next week	raishuu
the week after next	saraishuu
this month	kongetsu
last month	sengetsu
the month before last	sensengetsu

next month	raigetsu
the month after next	saraigetsu
this year	kotoshi
last year	kyonen
the year before last	ototoshi
next year	rainen
the year after next	sarainen
weekend	shuumatsu
morning	asa
A. M.	Gozen
noon	shoogo
P. M.	Gogo
afternoon	gogo
evening	yuugata
night	yoru
midnight	yonaka
exactly at six o'clock	rokuji choodo

Positions

up, on	ue

down, under	shita
middle, center	mannaka
right	migi
left	hidari
front, forward	mae
rear, back	ushiro
outside	soto
inside	naka
there	asoko
here	koko

Directions

north	kita
south	minami
east	higashi
west	nishi

Months

January	Ichigatsu
February	Nigatsu
March	Sangatsu
April	Shigatsu

May	Gogatsu
June	Rokugatsu
July	Shichigatsu
August	Hachigatsu
September	Kugatsu
October	Juugatsu
November	Juuichigatsu
December	Juunigatsu

Days of the month

1 (st)	tsuitachi
2 (nd)	futsuka
3 (rd)	mikka
4 (th)	yokka
5 (th)	itsuka
6 (th)	muika
7 (th)	nanoka
8 (th)	yooka
9 (th)	kokonoka
10 (th)	tooka
11 (th)	juuichinichi
12 (th)	juuninichi

13(th)	juusannichi
14(th)	juuyokka
15(th)	juugonichi
16(th)	juurokunichi
17(th)	juushichinichi
18(th)	juuhachinichi
19(th)	juukunichi
20(th)	hatsuka
24(th)	nijuuyokka
30(th)	sanjuunichi
31(th)	sanjuuichinichi

Days of the week

Sunday	Nichiyoobi
Monday	Getsuyoobi
Tuesday	Kayoobi
Wednesday	Suiyoobi
Thursday	Mokuyoobi
Friday	Kin'yoobi
Saturday	Doyoobi

Seasons

spring	haru
fall, autumn	aki
summer	natsu
winter	fuyu

Weather

rainy	ame
cloudy	kumori
fine	hare
snowy	yuki
thunder	kaminari
earthquake	jishin
typhoon	taifuu
windy	kaze

National holidays

national holiday	saijitsu
New Year's Day	Ganjitsu [Jan. 1]
Coming-of-Age Day	Seejin-no hi [Jan. 15]
National Founda-	Kenkoku kinenbi [Feb. 11]

tion Day

Vernal Equinox Day	Shunbun-no hi [March 20 or 21]
Constitution Day	Kenpoo kinenbi [May 3]
National Holiday	Kokumin-no kyuujitsu [May 4]
Children's Day	Kodomo-no hi [May 5]
Respect-for-the-Aged Day	Keiroo-no hi [Sep. 15]
Autumnal Equinox Day	Shuubun-no hi [Sep. 23 or 24]
Health-Sports Day	Taiiku-no hi [Oct. 10]
Culture Day	Bunka-no hi [Nov. 3]
Labor Thanksgiving Day	Kinroo Kansha-no hi [Nov.23]
Emperor's Birthday	Tennoo tanjoobi [Dec. 23]

Colors

red	aka
pink	pinku, momoiro
orange	orenjiiro, daidaiiro
yellow	kiiro

brown	chairo
green	midori
blue	ao
sky blue	mizuiro
purple	murasakiiro
wine red	azukiiro (wain reddo)
gray	haiiro, nezumiiro
black	kuro
white	shiro
silver	gin'iro
gold	kin'iro

Order

first	ichibanme
second	nibanme
third	sanbanme
fourth	yonbanme
fifth	gobanme
sixth	rokubanme
seventh	nanabanme
eighth	hachibanme
ninth	kyuubanme

tenth	juubanme
eleventh	juuichibanme
twelfth	juunibanme
thirteenth	juusanbanme
fourteenth	juuyonbanme
fifteenth	juugobanme
sixteenth	juurokubanme
seventeenth	juunanabanme
eighteenth	juuhachibanme
nineteenth	juukyuubanme
twentieth	nijuubanme
twenty-first	nijuuichibanme
twenty-second	nijuunibanme
thirtieth	sanjuubanme
fortieth	yonjuubanme
fiftieth	gojuubanme
sixtieth	rokujuubanme
seventieth	nanajuubanme
eightieth	hachijuubanme
ninetieth	kyujuubanme
hundredth	hyakubanme

Counting —— general

How many ?	Ikutsu desu-ka.
1	hitotsu
2	futatsu
3	mittsu
4	yottsu
5	itsutsu
6	muttsu
7	nanatsu
8	yattsu
9	kokonotsu
10	too

> To express any number above 10 for general counting purposes, use the cardinal number.

11	juuichi
12	juuni
20	nijuu

Counting —— frequency

How many times ~ ?	Nan-kai desu-ka.

1 (time)	ikkai
2	nikai
3	sankai
4	yonkai
5	gokai
6	rokkai
7	nanakai
8	hachikai
9	kyuukai
10	jukkai

Counting —— people

How many people ~?	Nan-nin desu-ka.
1 (person)	hitori
2	futari
3	sannin
4	yonin
5	gonin
6	rokunin
7	shichinin
8	hachinin

9	kyuunin
10	juunin
11	juuichinin
12	juuninin
20	nijuunin

Counting —— months / weeks

How long will you stay in Japan?	Dono-kurai nihon-ni iru yotei desu-ka.
About a month.	Ikkagetsu-gurai(desu).
Two months.	Nikagetsu.
Three months.	Sankagetsu.
Four months.	Yonkagetsu.
Five months.	Gokagetsu.
Six months.	Rokkagetsu.
Seven months.	Nanakagetsu.
Eight months.	Hachikagetsu.
Nine months.	Kyuukagetsu.
Ten months.	Jikkagetsu./Jukkagetsu.
One week.	Isshuukan(desu).
Two weeks.	Nishuukan.
Three weeks.	Sanshuukan.

Four weeks.	Yonshuukan.
Five weeks.	Goshuukan.
Six weeks.	Rokushuukan.
Seven weeks.	Nanashuukan.
Eight weeks.	Hasshuukan.
Nine weeks.	Kyuushuukan.
Ten weeks.	Jisshuukan./Jusshuukan.

Counting —— money

How much ∼ ?	Ikura desu-ka.
100 yen	Hyaku-en (desu).
200 yen	nihyaku-en
300 yen	sanbyaku-en
400 yen	yonhyaku-en
500 yen	gohyaku-en
600 yen	roppyaku-en
700 yen	nanahyaku-en
780 yen	nanahyaku-hachijuu-en
800 yen	happyaku-en
900 yen	kyuuhyaku-en
1,000 yen	sen-en
2,000 yen	nisen-en

3,000 yen	sanzen-en
4,000 yen	yonsen-en
5,000 yen	gosen-en
6,000 yen	rokusen-en
6,700 yen	rokusen-nanahyaku-en
7,000 yen	nanasen-en
8,000 yen	hassen-en
10,000 yen	ichiman-en
47,000 yen	yonman-nanasen-en
100,000 yen	juuman-en
180,000 yen	juuhachiman-en
500,000 yen	gojuuman-en
1,000,000 yen	hyakuman-en

Counting —— thin, flat objects (tickets, postage stamps, sheets of paper, etc.)

How many stamps ～?	Nan-mai desu-ka.
1 (stamp)	ichimai
2	nimai
3	sanmai
4	yonmai

5	gomai
6	rokumai
7	nanamai
8	hachimai
9	kyuumai
10	juumai

Counting —— long, slender objects (pencils, tubes, bottles, etc.)

How many pencils ~?	Nan-bon desu-ka.
1 (pencil)	ippon
2	nihon
3	sanbon
4	yonhon
5	gohon
6	roppon
7	nanahon
8	happon, hachihon
9	kyuuhon
10	jippon, juppon

Counting —— floors

What floor ~ ?	Nan-gai desu-ka.
1st floor	ikkai
2nd floor	nikai
3rd floor	sangai
4th floor	yonkai
5th floor	gokai
6th floor	rokkai
7th floor	nanakai
8th floor	hachikai
9th floor	kyuukai
10th floor	jikkai/jukkai
basement	chika
roof	okujoo

Fractions

half	hanbun
one half	nibun-no ichi
one third	sanbun-no ichi
quarter	yonbun-no ichi

Miscellaneous

one pair	hito-kumi
a dozen	ichi-daasu

USEFUL PHRASES

Daijoobu-desu. ╱ Mondai arimasen.
(That's O. K. ╱ No problem. ╱ Never mind.)

―――――― *INFORMATION* ――――――

★Dial 119 (Ambulance)

★You can buy various medicines at most pharmacies.

★You can apply for health insurance at the Ward Office near your home.

II

Situational
Words and Phrases

Subway

1. Hotel

Looking for a hotel

1. Could you suggest a good place to stay? — Ii shukuhakusaki-o oshiete-itadakemasu-ka.

2. Could you suggest a good hotel? — Ii hoteru-o shookai-shite-itadakemasu-ka.

3. Are there any hotels near Narita airport? — Narita-kuukoo-no chikaku-ni hoteru-ga arimasu-ka.

4. Do I need a reservation? — Yoyaku-ga irimasu-ka.

5. Can I stay at that hotel without a reservation? — Yoyaku-shinai-de sono hoteru-ni tomaremasu-ka.

Making reservations

1. I'd like to reserve a room. — Heya-o yoyaku-shitai-no-desu.

2. Do you have a room available? — Heya-wa aite-imasu-ka.

3. Do you have a dou- — Daburu-no heya-ga

ble?

arimasu-ka.

4. A single with a bath, please.

Basu-tsuki shinguru-o onegai-shimasu.

5. We'd like to have rooms for four people on October 2nd.

Juugatsu futsuka-ni yonin tomaritai-no-desu.

6. I'll be staying for two nights.

Nihaku-no yotee desu.

7. Do you have any better rooms?

Motto ii heya-ga arimasu-ka.

8. Do you have multiple-bed rooms?

Oozee tomareru heya-wa arimasu-ka.

9. We're a party of eight.

Hachinin-no dantai-desu.

10. Please don't cancel my reservation.

Yoyaku-o torikesanaide-kudasai.

11. I'll arrive at the hotel around ten thirty tonight.

Kon'ya juu-ji-han-goro hoteru-ni tsukimasu.

12. Is breakfast includ-

Chooshoku-tsuki desu-

ed ?   ka.

Asking about room rates

1. What's the room rate ?   Heya-dai-wa ikura desu-ka.

2. Is tax included ?   Zeekomi desu-ka.

3. How about service charge ?   Saabisu-ryoo-wa doo-natte-imasu-ka.

4. Is this the room rate only ?   Sono ryookin-wa shukuhakuryoo-dakedesu-ka.

5. It's a little too expensive for us.   Watashi-tachi-niwa chotto taka-sugimasu.

6. I'd rather have a less expensive one.   Motto yasui heya-no hoo-ga ii-desu.

7. I'd like to have a room for under thirty dollars a night.   Ippaku sanjuu-doru-ika-no heya-ni shitai-no-desu.

Checking in

1. I have a reservation for a single room.

   Shinguru-no heya-o yoyaku-shite-arimasu.

2. I made a reservation from Kyoto.

   Kyooto-kara yoyaku-shimashita.

3. I made a call from the airport.

   Kuukoo-kara denwa-shimashita.

4. I don't have a reservation.

   Yoyaku-shite-arimasen.

5. I'm sure I have a reservation.

   Tashika-ni yoyaku-shite-arimasu.

6. Will you try to find my name again?

   Moo ichido namae-o sagashite-kudasai.

7. Shall I show you my passport?

   Pasupooto-o omise-shimashoo-ka.

8. Do I sign here?

   Koko-ni shomee-suru-no-desu-ka.

9. Do I have to order breakfast now?

   Ima chooshoku-o tanomanakereba ikemasen-ka.

10. What time is breakfast ?   Chooshoku-wa nan-ji
     desu-ka.

11. When does the coffee shop open ?   Kissashitsu-wa itsu
     akimasu-ka.

12. When does it close ?   Itsu shimarimasu-ka.

13. When is the checkout time ?   Chekku-auto-wa nan-ji
     desu-ka.

Hotel services

1. May I have room service ?   Ruumu-saabisu-o
     onegai-dekimasu-ka.

2. My room number is 706.   Heya-no bangoo-wa
     706 (nana-zero-roku)
     desu.

3. Will you bring the breakfast t o my room ?   Chooshoku-o heya-ni
     todokete-moraemasu-
     ka.

4. Coffee, too, please.   Koohii-mo onegai-
     shimasu.

5. May I have another   Moo ichimai moofu-o

blanket ?	itadakemasu-ka.
6. I'd like to make an international phone call.	Kokusai-denwa-ga kaketai-no-desu.
7. Do you have a laundry service ?	Kuriiningu-no-saabisu-wa arimasu-ka.
8. Where is the laundry service ?	Kuriiningu-no-saabisu-wa doko desu-ka.
9. When will it be ready ?	Itsu dekimasu-ka.
10. How much will it be ?	Ikura-ni narimasu-ka.
11. When should I pay for it ?	Ryookin-wa itsu oshiharai-sureba ii-desu-ka.
12. Can it be done quickly ?	Isoide-moraemasu-ka.
13. Will you cash my check, please.	Kogitte-o genkin-ni kaete-moraemasu-ka.
14. May I leave a mes-	843 (Hachi-yon-san)

sage for Mr.Yamada in room 843 ?	gooshitsu-no Yamada-san-ni dengon-o onegai-dekimasu-ka.
15. Are there any messages for me ?	Watashi-ni dengon-ga arimasu-ka.
16. Could you give me a wake up call ?	Mooningu-kooru-o onegai-dekimasu-ka.
17. Will you wake me up at seven tomorrow morning ?	Asu-no-asa shichiji-ni mooningu-kooru-o onegai-dekimasu-ka.
18. Could you keep this for me ?	Kore-o azukatte-kudasai.
19. May I leave my baggage until I check in later ?	Nochi-hodo chekku-in-suru-toki-made, nimotsu-o oiteoite-mo yoroshii-desu-ka.

Complaints, requests, etc.

1. The toilet won't stop flushing.	Toire-no mizu-ga tomarimasen.

2. The TV set doesn't seem to work well.

Terebi-no chooshi-ga warui-yoo-desu.

3. The hot water isn't running.

Oyu-ga demasen.

4. Water doesn't come out of the shower.

Shawaa-no mizu-ga demasen.

5. The shower water's too hot.

Shawaa-no oyu-ga atsu-sugi-masu.

6. The light in the bathroom doesn't work.

Yokushitsu-no denki-ga tsukimasen.

7. There is no towel in the bathroom.

Yokushitsu-ni taoru-ga arimasen.

8. Will you tell me how to adjust it?

Choosetsu-no hoohoo-o oshiete-kudasai.

9. Could you come and fix it?

Shuuri-ni kite-morae-masu-ka.

10. The people next door are too loud.

Tonari-no heya-ga sugoku sawagashii-desu.

11. My laundry hasn't

Sentakumono-ga mada

come yet.	kite-imasen.
12. The door won't lock.	Doa-no kagi-ga kakaranai-yoo-desu.
13. Could you explain how to lock the door?	Kagi-no kake-kata-o setsumee-shite-itadake-masu-ka.
14. I've locked myself out of my room.	Heya-ni kagi-o wasureta-mama shimete-shimai-mashita.
15. The window of my room doesn't close.	Heya-no mado-ga shimarimasen.
16. The air conditioning doesn't work.	Reiboo-ga kiite-imasen.
17. Who is it?	Donata desu-ka.

Checking out

| 1. I'm leaving tomorrow. | Ashita, tachimasu. |
| 2. I'm going to check out at seven tomor- | Asu-no-asa shichiji-ni chekku-auto-suru- |

row morning.	tsumori-desu.
3. I'm going to leave one day earlier than planned.	Yotee-yori ichinichi hayaku tachimasu.
4. I'd like to stay one more night.	Moo ippaku shitai-no-desu.
5. Can I extend my stay two more days?	Moo futsuka shukuhaku-o enchoo-dekimasu-ka.
6. Can I pay in dollars?	Doru-de haratte-mo ii-desu-ka.
7. Will you call me a cab, please?	Takushii-o yonde-itadakemasu-ka.
8. I forgot something in the room.	Heya-ni wasuremono-o shimashita.

Hotel

Japanese style hotel	ryokan
reception	uketsuke
name	namae
room number	heya-no bangoo
heated/air conditioned	reidanboo-kanbi
with bath and toilet	basu-toire-tsuki
with two meals	ippaku-nishoku-tsuki
Western style room	yooshitsu
Japanese style room	washitsu
bath	yokushitsu, ofuro
bath for a few people	kazoku-buro
outdoor hot spring bath	roten-buro
hot spring	onsen
key	kagi
toilet	otearai, toire

bed (Western style)	beddo
bed (Japanese style)	futon
blanket	moofu
pillow	makura
sheet	shiitsu
quilt	kakebuton
stairs	kaidan
emergency exit	hijooguchi
breakfast	chooshoku, asagohan
lunch	chuushoku, hirugohan
supper	yuushoku, yuugohan
laundry	sentaku
dry cleaning	dorai-kuriiningu
cancel	kyanseru, torikeshi

2. Bank, Exchange

Looking for a bank

1. Where is a bank ? Ginkoo-wa doko desu-
ka.

2. Where is the near- Ichiban chikai ginkoo-wa
est bank ? doko desu-ka.

3. What time do Ginkoo-wa nan-ji-ni
banks open? hirakimasu-ka.

4. Are banks open on Ginkoo-wa doyoobi-mo
Saturdays, too ? aite-imasu-ka.

At the counter

1. I want to open an Kooza-ga hirakitai-desu.
account.

2. I want to have trav- Ryokoo-kogitte-ga
eller's checks made. tsukuritai-desu.

3. Please go to the 2nd Nikai-e doozo.
floor.

4. Please tell me how Kono yooshi-no
to fill in this form. kakikata-o oshiete-
itadake-masu-ka.

5. Please sign here.   Koko-ni sain-shite-kudasai.

6. Please correct it.   Teesee-shite-kudasai.

7. Please make sure it's right.   Kakunin-shite-kudasai.

8. I have a check.   Kogitte-o motte-imasu.

9. I have a credit card.   Kurejitto-kaado-ga arimasu.

10. I don't have cash.   Genkin-wa motte-imasen.

11. I don't have a seal.   Inkan-o motte-imasen.

12. Do I have to show my passport?   Pasupooto-o omise-shinakereba ikemasen-ka.

13. Is this the form to transfer money to a person's account?   Kore-wa furikomi-no yooshi desu-ka.

Withdrawing money (at a bank machine)

1. Please tell me how   Kono kikai-no tsukai-

to use this machine.	kata-o oshiete-kudasai.
2. The money doesn't come out.	Okane-ga demasen.
3. I forgot my secret code.	Anshoo-bangoo-o wasuremashita.
4. I've lost my cash card.	Kyasshu-kaado-o nakushimashita.
5. Please reissue my cash card.	Kyasshu-kaado-o saihakkoo-shite-kudasai.
6. I have my bank account number.	Ginkoo-no kooza-bangoo-wa hikaete-arimasu.

Exchange (1)

1. Where can I change money ?	Doko-de ryoogae dekimasu-ka.
2. Will you change money for me ?	Ryoogae-shite-itadake-masu-ka.
3. How much will it be	En desu-to ikura-ni

in yen?	narimasu-ka.
4. How many yen to the dollar?	Ichi-doru-wa ikura desu-ka.
5. What is the exchange rate?	Kookan-reeto-wa ikura desu-ka.
6. What's the exchange rate for the dollar today?	Kyoo-no doru-no reeto-wa ikura desu-ka.
7. I want to change some dollars into yen.	Doru-o en-ni kaetai-desu.
8. Please cash this 100 dollars' check for yen.	Kono 100 (hyaku)-doru -no kogitte-o en-no genkin-ni kaete-kudasai.
9. Will you cash these U.S. dollars checks?	Kono amerika-doru-no kogitte-o genkin-ni shite-itadakemasu-ka.

Exchange (2)

1. Please break this 10,000 yen bill.	Ichiman-en-o kuzushite-kudasai.

2. Please change this into 1,000 yen notes.

Sen-en-satsu-ni kuzushite-kudasai.

3. Could you break this five thousand yen bill?

Kono gosen-en-satsu-o kuzushite-itadakemasu-ka.

4. I'd like to break this one thousand yen bill into coins.

Kono sen-en-satsu-o kozeni-ni kaetai-no-desu.

5. I'd like to break this ten thousand yen bill into thousand yen bills.

Kono ichiman-en-satsu-o sen-en-satsu-ni kaetai-no-desu.

6. I want some small change too, please.

Kozeni-mo hoshii-desu.

Remittance

1. I would like to remit this money to India.

Indo-ni sookin-shitai-no-desu.

2. I'd like to get the

Itaria-kara-no sookin-o

money sent from
Italy.

uketoritai-no-desu.

3. Can I get the money
by tomorrow noon ?

Ashita-no hiru-made-ni
okane-ga todokimasu-
ka.

4. I would like to
transfer this money.

Okane-o furikomitai-no-
desu.

Miscellaneous

1. Can I pay in Amer-
ican dollars in this
country ?

Kono kuni-de amerika-
doru-wa tsuuyoo-
shimasu-ka.

2. Can you accept a
dollar check ?

Doru-no kogitte-wa
atsukatte-imasu-ka.

3. I want to know my
balance.

Zandaka-shookai-ga
shitai-desu.

4. How much is the
commission ?

Tesuuryoo-wa ikura
desu-ka.

Bank, Exchange

bank (Fuji bank)	ginkoo (Fuji ginkoo)
check	kogitte
traveler's check	ryokoosha-yoo-kogitte／toraberaazu-chekku
foreign exchange, international money order	gaikokukawase
bank account	ginkoo-kooza
deposit (at a bank)	yokin [ginkoo-yokin]
withdrawal	hikidashi
bankbook	tsuuchoo
interest	rishi
money	okane
small coins	komakai-okane／kozeni
note, bill	osatsu
teller	madoguchigakari
branch	shiten
cash card, money card	kyasshu kaado
money machine	genkin-jidoo-shiharaiki／kyasshu disupensaa

ATM, automatic teller machine	genkin-jidoo-azukeire-shiharaiki
automatic withdrawal	jidoo-hikiotoshi
remittance	sookin
balance	zandaka
fee	tesuuryoo
exchange	ryoogae
currency	tsuuka
foreign exchange rate	kawase-reeto
yen	en
dollar	doru
pound	pondo
franc	furan
transfer	furikomi

Automatic Teller Machine

3. Restaurant

Looking for a restaurant

1. I want something to eat.	Nani-ka tabetai-desu.
2. Can you suggest a good restaurant?	Ii resutoran-o shookai-shite-itadakemasu-ka.
3. Is there an inexpensive restaurant near here?	Kono chikaku-ni amari takakunai resutoran-ga arimasu-ka.
4. Are there any Japanese restaurants around here?	Kono atari-ni nihon-ryooriten-ga arimasu-ka.
5. I'd like to have some Japanese food for dinner.	Yuushoku-niwa nihon-ryoori-ga tabetai-no-desu.

Reservations

1. I'd like to make a reservation, please.	Yoyaku-o onegai-shimasu.
2. Do we need a reservation?	Yoyaku-ga hitsuyoo-desu-ka.

| 3. We'd like a table for four at seven o'clock. | Shichiji-ni yonin-bun-no seki-o onegai-shimasu. |

Asking about service

1. Are you open?	Eegyoochuu desu-ka.
2. What time do you start serving dinner?	Yuushoku-wa nan-ji-kara desu-ka.
3. May I have breakfast now?	Ima chooshoku-o tanomemasu-ka.
4. Can we have just coffee here?	Koohii-o nomu-dake-demo kamaimasen-ka.

Being seated

1. Welcome.	Irasshaimase.
2. How many are there in your party?	Nan-mee-sama desu-ka.
3. We're a party of seven.	Shichinin-desu.
4. Can we have a	Seki-wa arimasu-ka.

table ?

5. May I take this seat ?	Kono seki-ni suwatte-mo ii-desu-ka.
6. Do you mind if I join you ?	Aiseki-sasete-itadaite-mo yoroshii-desu-ka.
7. Please come this way.	Kochira-e doozo.
8. There are no seats available now.	Tadaima manseki-desu.
9. When can we get a table ?	Itsu-goro seki-ga akimasu-ka.

Ordering

1. May I see a menu ?	Menyuu-o misete-itadakemasu-ka.
2. Do you have a menu written in English ?	Eego-no menyuu-wa arimasu-ka.
3. What would you like ?	Nani-ni nasaimasu-ka.

4. I'll take ~./Please give me ~.

~-ni shimasu./~-o kudasai.

5. Do you have ~?

~ wa arimasuka.

6. I haven't made up my mind yet.

Mada kimete-imasen.

7. What kinds of beer do you have?

Donna shurui-no biiru-ga arimasu-ka.

8. A bottle of wine, please.

Wain-o ippon onegai-shimasu.

9. What do you suggest?

Osusumehin-wa nan desu-ka.

10. Could you recommend something else?

Nani-ka hoka-ni osusume hin-wa arimasu-ka.

11. What are the local specialties?

Koko-no kyoodoryoori-wa nan desu-ka.

12. What's this made of?

Kore-no zairyoo-wa nan desu-ka.

13. What does it taste like?

Sore-wa donoyoo-na aji desu-ka.

14. What can you serve quickly?   Hayaku dekiru mono-wa nan desu-ka.

15. May I order now?   Ima chuumon-shite-mo yoroshii-desu-ka.

16. I'll order dessert later.   Dezaato-wa ato-de chuumon-shimasu.

17. I'd like to order the same.   Onaji-mono-ga chuumon-shitai-no-desu.

18. What do you have for dessert?   Dezaato-wa nani-ga arimasu-ka.

19. Is this sweet?   Kore-wa amai desu-ka.

20. I'll have coffee after dinner.   Shokugo-ni koohii-o onegai-shimasu.

21. May I have coffee instead of tea?   Koocha-no kawari-ni Koohii-o mottekite-itadakemasu-ka.

22. With cream and sugar, please.   Miruku-to satoo-o irete-kudasai.

At the table

1. I didn't order this.
Kore-wa chuumon-
shite-imasen.

2. This tastes strange.
Hen-na aji-ga shimasu.

3. It's delicious.
Totemo oishii-desu.

4. My vegetable salad
hasn't come yet.
Yasai-sarada-ga mada
kimasen.

5. Could you tell me
the proper way to eat
this?
Joozu-na tabekata-o
oshiete-itadakemasu-ka.

6. Give me a knife and
fork, please.
Naifu-to fooku-o
kudasai.

7. I dropped my chop-
sticks.
Ohashi-o otoshite-
shimaimashita.

8. Would you pass the
salt, please?
Shio-o totte-
itadakemasu-ka.

9. Would you bring
me ~?
~-o mottekite-
itadakemasu-ka.

10. Would you like
some more?
Moo sukoshi ikaga desu-
ka.

11. I've had enough.　　　Juubun itadakimashita./
　　　　　　　　　　　　Onaka-ga ippai-ni
　　　　　　　　　　　　narimashita.

12. No, thank you.　　　　Iie kekkoo-desu.

13. No more, thanks.　　　Moo kekkoo-desu.

14. I cannot eat ～.　　　～-o taberukoto-ga
　　　　　　　　　　　　dekimasen.

15. May I have some　　Suupu-o moo sukoshi
　　more soup?　　　　itadakemasu-ka.

16. May I have another　Koohii-o moo ippai
　　cup of coffee?　　　itadakemasu-ka.

17. May I smoke?　　　　Tabako-o sutte-mo
　　　　　　　　　　　　ii-desu-ka.

Paying the bill

1. May I have the bill,　Okanjoo-o onegai-
　　please?　　　　　　shimasu.

2. We'd like to pay　　Betsubetsu-ni haraitai-
　　separately.　　　　no-desu.

3. Where should I　　Doko-de harau-no desu-

pay?	ka.
4. Does this include a service charge?	Saabisuryoo-wa haitte-imasu-ka.
5. Can I pay in U.S. dollars?	Doru-de haraukoto-ga dekimasu-ka.
6. Do you accept traveler's checks here?	Koko-de toraberaazu-chekku-ga tsukaemasu-ka.
7. Keep the change, please.	Otsuri-wa totteoite-kudasai.

Light meals

1. How do I order?	Dono yoo-ni chuumon-suru-no-desu-ka.
2. Do I need to buy a food ticket first?	Saki-ni shokken-o kau-no-desu-ka.
3. Should I pay first?	Saki-ni harau-no-desu-ka.
4. Take out, please.	Mochikaerimasu.

Box lunches (obentoo)

1. What kind of box lunches do you have ?

Donna obentoo-ga arimasu-ka.

2. We have nine types of box lunches.

Kyuushurui-no obentoo-ga arimasu.

3. Which is the cheapest box lunch ?

Ichiban yasui obentoo-wa dore desu-ka.

4. Please give me only rice.

Raisu-dake kudasai.

5. I want three orders of rice.

Gohan-ga mittsu hoshii-desu.

6. Please give me a cup of miso-soup.

Omisoshiru-o tsukete-kudasai.

7. Please give me a large order of rice.

Gohan-o oomori-ni shite-kudasai.

Restaurants

restaurant	shokudoo, resutoran
coffee shop	kissaten
McDonald's	makudonarudo
buckwheat noodle shop	sobaya
grilled meat shop	yakinikuya
snack bar	sunakku
bar	nomiya
stand	yatai
open	eegyoochuu
closed	junbichuu, heiten
service charge	saabisuryo
tax	zeekin
reservation	yoyaku
order	chuumon
matches	matchi
ashtray	haizara
chair	isu

Types of cuisine

Japanese (cuisine)	nihonryoori

Chinese	chuukaryoori
Korean	kankokuryoori
French	furansuryoori
Italian	itariaryoori
local	kyoodoryoori
vegetarian	yasairyoori
vegetarian (traditional)	shoojinryoori
simple meal served before a ceremonial tea	kaiseki-ryoori

Meals

food	tabemono
meal	shokuji
breakfast	asagohan, chooshoku
lunch	hirugohan, ohiru, chuushoku
dinner	yuugohan, yuushoku
box lunch	obentoo
snack between lunch and supper	oyatsu

Food names

appetizer	tsumami, oodoburu
soup	suupu
salad	sarada
deep-fried shrimp	ebi-furai
curry and rice	karee-raisu
spaghetti	supagettii
steak	suteeki
breaded pork cut-let	tonkatsu
breaded chicken cutlet	chikinkatsu
hamburger	hanbaagaa
hamburger steak	hanbaagu
sandwich	sandoitchi
grilled meat	yakiniku
set menu, table d'hôte	teeshoku
boiled egg	yudetamago
sunny-side up, fried eggs	medamayaki
ham and eggs	hamueggu

omelette	omuretsu
miso soup	misoshiru
sushi (sliced raw fish and rice)	sushi
sliced raw fish	sashimi
tempura (fried fish or vegetables)	tenpura
rice with cooked tempura on top	tendon
rice with chicken and egg on top	oyakodon
barbecued chicken	yakitori
boiled rice	gohan
rice ball	onigiri
bread	pan
buckwheat noodle, Japanese noodle	soba
white noodle	udon
Chinese noodle	raamen
frozen food	reetoo-shokuhin
cake	keeki
ice cream	aisukuriim

pancake	hottokeeki
bean cake	wagashi
rice cracker	osenbee

Box lunches

box lunch	obentoo
box lunch with dried seaweed	noribentoo
salmon box lunch	sakebentoo
eel box lunch	unagibentoo
rice ball with salmon	sake-no onigiri
rice ball with pickled plum	ume-no onigiri
rice ball with dried bonito	okaka-no onigiri

Drinks

drink	nomimono
water	mizu
hot water	oyu
coffee	koohii

tea	koocha
cocoa	kokoa
milk	miruku, gyuunyuu
Japanese green tea	ocha, ryokucha
juice	juusu
soda	sooda
alcohol	osake
Japanese sake	nihonshu
beer	biiru
canned beer	kanbiiru
bottled beer	binbiiru
draft beer	namabiiru
whiskey	uisukii
brandy	burandee
wine	wain
dry	karakuchi
light, sweet	amakuchi

Vegetables

vegetables	yasai
carrot	ninjin
onion	tamanegi

green pepper	piiman
potato	poteto, jagaimo
tomato	tomato
cucumber	kyuuri
cabbage	kyabetsu
corn	koon, toomorokoshi
celery	serori
bean	mame
pumpkin	kabocha
spinach	hoorensoo
lettuce	retasu
mushroom	masshuruumu
asparagus	asuparagasu
broccoli	burokkorii
cauliflower	karifurawaa
Japanese mush-room	shiitake
ginger	shooga
Japanese leek	naganegi
garlic	ninniku

Fruits

fruit	furuutsu, kudamono
mandarin orange	mikan
orange	orenji
lemon	remon
apple	ringo
grape	budoo
strawberry	ichigo
banana	banana
grapefruit	gureepu-furuutsu
peach	momo
cherry	sakuranbo
persimmon	ka$\overline{\text{ki}}$
watermelon	suika
pear	nashi
fig	ichijiku

Meat

meat	niku
beef	gyuuniku
pork	butaniku
chicken	toriniku

mutton	maton
tongue	tan
minced meat (beef and pork)	aibiki
minced meat	hikiniku
liver	rebaa

Seafood

fish	sakana
sardine	iwashi
salmon	sake
horse mackerel	aji
bonito	katsuo
tuna	maguro
flatfish	hirame
codfish	tara
trout	masu
herring	nishin
cuttlefish, squid	ika
octopus	tako
shrimp	ebi
lobster	ise-ebi

crab	kani
oyster	kaki
shell, shellfish	kai
clam	asari
corbicula	shijimi
scallop	hotategai
eel	unagi
mudfish	dojoo

Miscellaneous

ham	hamu
egg	tamago
bean curd	toofu
rice cake	omochi
dried seaweed	nori

Spices, etc.

salt	shio
sugar	shugaa, satoo
soy sauce	shooyu
sauce	soosu
bean paste	miso

vinegar	su, osu
spice	kooshinryoo
pepper	koshoo
butter	bataa
margarine	maagarin
cheese	chiizu
oil	abura
mayonnaise	mayoneezu
jam	jamu
marmalade	maamareedo

Cooking methods

roast, grill, bake, toast	yaku
boil, cook, simmer	niru
boil (put something into hot water)	yuderu
deep-fry	ageru
steam	musu
fry (lightly)	itameru

Tableware, cooking implements

plate	sara
glass	koppu/gurasu
cup	kappu
rice bowl	chawan
Japanese tea cup	yunomi
Japanese small tea pot	kyuusu
knife	naifu
fork	fooku
spoon	supuun
can opener	kankiri
bottle opener	sennuki
coaster	koosutaa
pot, saucepan	nabe
chopsticks	ohashi
chopstick holder	hashioki
toothpick	yooji
frying pan	furaipan
kitchen knife	hoochoo
chopping board	manaita
air-tight jar	potto

4. Shopping

Looking for a shop

1. Could you recommend a good shop?

   Ii mise-o shitte-imasu-ka.

2. Where can I get an English paper?

   Eejishinbun-wa doko-de kaemasu-ka.

3. Where's the biggest bookshop around here?

   Konohen-de ichiban ookii shoten-wa doko desu-ka.

4. Is there a discount shop around here?

   Konohen-ni disukaunto-shoppu-ga arimasu-ka.

5. Can I get daily necessities in that store?

   Ano mise-de nichiyoohin-o kaukoto-ga dekimasu-ka.

Addressing a customer

1. Welcome.

   Irasshaimase.

2. What are you looking for?

   Nani-o osagashi desu-ka.

3. What would you like to buy?

   Nani-ni nasaimasu-ka.

4. How would you like ~?   ~-wa ikaga-desu-ka.

5. Wait a moment, please.   Shooshoo omachi-kudasai.

6. Certainly.   Kashikomarimashita.

7. About how much would you like to spend?   Goyosan-wa.

8. Have you decided?   Okimari desu-ka.

9. I'm sorry, but we don't carry them.   Mooshiwake-arimasen. Tooten-niwa arimasen.

10. I'm sorry, but it's out of stock.   Ainiku urikire desu.

Addressing a clerk

1. Excuse me. Could you help me?   Sumimasen. Onegai-shimasu.

2. Do you have ~?   ~-wa arimasu-ka.

3. Do you have a clerk who can speak Eng-   Eego-no wakaru ten'insan-wa imasu-ka.

lish?

4. I need some socks.	Kutsushita-ga hoshii-desu.
5. I'd like to see some cigarette cases.	Shigaretto-keesu-o misete-kudasai.
6. Please look for it.	Sagashite-kudasai.

Asking about specific items

1. What's this for?	Nani-ni tsukau-no desu-ka.
2. Will you explain how to do that, please?	Donoyoo-ni suruno-ka setsumee-shite-itadakemasu-ka.
3. Are there English instructions to go with it?	Eego-no setsumeesho-ga tsuite-imasu-ka.
4. What's it made of?	Sore-wa nani-de dekite-iru-no-desu-ka.
5. What kind of leather is it?	Nan-no kawa desu-ka.

6. Is this a waterproof watch?

Kore-wa boosuidokee desu-ka.

7. Please explain this word-processer.

Kono waapuro-ni-tsuite setsumee-shite-kudasai.

8. Can I use this appliance in the United States?

Kono denkiseehin-wa amerika-de tsukaukoto-ga dekimasu-ka.

9. Is this for women or men?

Kore-wa fujinyoo desu-ka, shinshiyoo desu-ka.

10. Can I return this?

Henpin dekimasu-ka.

Making a decision

1. How do you like it?

Ikaga desu-ka.

2. Please give me this.

Kore-o kudasai.

3. Will you keep this for me?

Kore-o totteoite-moraemasu-ka.

4. I'll come back and get it later because I don't have enough money with me.

Mochiawase-ga arimasen-node ato-de kainikimasu.

5. I can't find what I want.　Hoshii mono-ga mitsukarimasen.

6. No, thanks.　Iie, kekkoo-desu.

7. I'll think about it, thank you.　Sukoshi kangaete-mimasu, arigatoo.

8. I can't decide now.　Mada kimete-imasen.

9. I'm just looking.　Miteiru-dake desu.

Asking for more selection

1. Can you show me something else?　Hoka-no mono-o misete-kudasai.

2. May I see something else in a different style?　Chigau dezain-no mono-o misete-itadakemasu-ka.

3. Do you have anything of better quality?　Motto shitsu-no ii mono-ga arimasu-ka.

4. Do you have the same thing in another color?　Hoka-no iro-ga arimasu-ka.

Asking about size

1. I don't know my size.

Saizu-ga wakarimasen.

2. Would you take my measurements?

Saizu-o hakatte-itadakemasu-ka.

3. May I try on this coat?

Kono kooto-o shichaku-shite-mo yoroshii-desu-ka.

4. This shirt doesn't fit me.

Kono shatsu-wa watashi-ni aimasen.

5. This jacket isn't my size.

Kono jaketto-wa saizu-ga aimasen.

6. It's too small.

Chiisa-sugimasu.

7. This is too big for me.

Kore-wa ooki-sugimasu.

8. Do you have a bigger [smaller] one?

Motto ookii [chiisai] mono-wa arimasu-ka.

9. Will you adjust the length?

Take-o naoshite-moraemasu-ka.

10. Could you adjust it

Imasugu naoshite-

right now? moraemasu-ka.

11. A little bit shorter, Moo chotto [sukoshi]
    please. mijikaku-shite-kudasai.

Asking about price

1. How much is this? Kore-wa ikura desu-ka.

2. How much are Kono shiitake-wa ichi-
   these mushrooms per kiroguramu ikura desu-
   kilogram? ka.

3. How much is it in Zenbu-de ikura desu-ka.
   total?

4. Does the price Kono nedan-wa zeekomi
   include tax? desu-ka.

5. Can I get it tax- Menzee-de kaemasu-ka.
   free?

6. Do you have any Ichiman-en zengo-no
   bags for around ten baggu-wa arimasu-ka.
   thousand yen?

7. Do you have any Hoka-ni onaji-yoo-na
   others for about the nedan-no mono-wa

same price ?	arimasu-ka.
8. Are these on sale today ?	Kore-wa nebiki-shitearu-no-desu-ka.
9. That's too expensive.	Taka-sugimasu.
10. I can't spend that much.	Sonna-ni yosan-ga arimasen.
11. Could you give me a discount ?	Nebiki-shite-moraemasu-ka.
12. Do you have anything cheaper ?	Motto yasui mono-wa arimasuka.
13. Please show me the cheapest one.	Ichiban yasui no-o misete-kudasai.

Paying

1. Where's the cashier, please ?	Okanjooba [Kyasshaa]-wa doko desu-ka.
2. Can I use this card ?	Kono kaado-wa tsukaemasu-ka.
3. Can I pay you in	Toraberaazu-chekku-de

traveler's checks?	haraemasu-ka.
4. May I pay by check?	Kogitte-de haratte-mo ii-desu-ka.
5. Can I pay by credit card?	Kurejitto-kaado-demo ii-desu-ka.
6. Yes, you can.	Hai, kekkoo-desu.
7. May I have a receipt, please?	Reshiito-o itadakemasu-ka.
8. May I have a written receipt, please?	Ryooshuusho-o itadakemasu-ka.

Delivery, repairs

1. Please deliver it.	Todokete-kudasai.
2. This is the address.	Juusho desu.
3. Can you send this to the United States?	Amerika-made okutte-moraemasu-ka.
4. Please send it to this address.	Koko-ni okutte-kudasai.
5. Do you charge for delivery?	Sooryoo-wa kakarimasu-ka.

6. Can you have this installed?   Toritsukete-moraemasu-ka.

7. Please fix this.   Naoshite-kudasai.

8. Can it be repaired by tomorrow?   Ashita-made-ni naori-masu-ka.

9. When will it be ready?   Itsu dekimasu-ka.

10. What time can it be done?   Nan-ji-ni dekimasu-ka.

11. How much will it cost?   Ikura kakari-masu-ka.

―――― INFORMATION ――――

★You can use international credit cards (Master card, Visa card, American Express, etc.) in many stores.

Shops, etc.

department store (Mitsukoshi department store)	depaato (*Ex*. Mitsukoshi depaato)
supermarket	suupaa-maaketto
discount shop	disukaunto shoppu
duty-free shop	menzeehinten
vegetable shop	yaoya
fish shop	sakanaya
bakery	pan'ya
butcher	nikuya
confectionery	okashiya
liquor store	sakaya
camera shop	kameraya
stationery store	bunbooguya
bookstore	hon'ya
florist	hanaya
drugstore	kusuriya
cosmetics shop	keshoohin'ya
antique shop	kottoohin'ya, antiiku-shoppu
toy shop	omochaya

folkcrafts shop	mingeehinten
souvenir shop	miyagemonoya
filling station	gasorin-sutando
art gallery	garoo (*Ex.* Nichidoo garoo)
beauty parlor	biyooin
barber shop	tokoya
tax free	menzee
duty-free	menzee
clerk	ten'in
person in charge	sekininsha
sale	seeru
elevator, lift	erebeetaa
escalator	esukareetaa
pamphlet	panfuretto
contents	naiyoo

Decorative objects, souvenirs

souvenir, present	omiyage
fan	sensu
Japanese lacquer ware	urushinuri
lacquer ware	shikki

hanging picture scroll	kakejiku
sword	katana
folding screen	byoobu
screen door, sliding screen	fusuma
Japanese style guitar	shamisen
tray	obon
pot	tsubo
porcelain	jiki
pottery	tooki
ceramics	toojiki
bamboo products	take-seehin
inlaying	zoogan
statue of Buddha	butsuzoo
ink painting	sumie
woodblock print of the Edo period	ukiyoe
short cotton curtain slit at intervals	noren

cloth wrapper	furoshiki
workman's coat	happi
two-toed cloth footwear	tabi
towel	tenugui
pearl	shinju
folkcraft	mingeehin
kite	tako
top	koma
drum	taiko
oilpaper umbrella	bangasa
picture	e
doll	ningyoo
music box	orugooru
toy	omocha
folding paper	origami
washi paper	washi
ornamental hairpin	kanzashi
jewelry	hooseki
accessaries	akusesarii
ring	yubiwa
earrings	iaringu

brooch	buroochi
pendant	pendanto
necklace	nekkuresu
glasses	megane
sunglasses	sangurasu
handbag	handobaggu

Clothing, etc.

clothes	iryoohin
dress	doresu, wanpiisu
suit	suutsu
kimono	kimono
broad sash tied over a kimono	obi
skirt	sukaato
T shirt	tiishatsu
blouse	burausu
shirt	waishatsu
business suit	sebiro
pants, trousers	zubon
coat	uwagi
blazer	burezaa

sweater	seetaa
jeans	jiipan, jiinzu
overcoat	oobaa
scarf	sukaafu
necktie	nekutai
gloves	tebukuro
nightdress	nemaki
swim suit	mizugi
socks	kutsushita, sokkusu
shoes	kutsu
sneakers	suniikaa
wooden clogs	geta
cap, hat	booshi
umbrella	kasa
underwear	shitagi
undershirt	shatsu
slip	surippu
shorts	shootsu
briefs	buriifu
panties	pantii
brassière	burajaa
stockings, panty	sutokkingu

hose

cotton	momen
silk	kinu
linen	asa
wool	yoomoo/
	uuru
polyester	poriesuteru
cashmere	kashimiya
plain	muji
pattern	gara, moyoo
check	chekku
tartan check	taatan-chekku
dot	mizutamamoyoo
stripe	shimamoyoo
block check	ichimatsumoyoo
print	purinto-gara
children's	kodomoyoo
men's	shinshiyoo
women's	fujinyoo
sleeve	sode
half sleeve	hansode
long sleeve	nagasode

short	mijikai
long	nagai
big, large	ookii
small	chiisai
tight	kitsui
loose	yurui
button	botan
scissors	hasami
thread, string	ito
needle, pin	hari
safety pins	anzen-pin
lining	uraji
collar	eri

Electrical appliances and accessories

electrical appliances	denki-seehin
record	rekoodo
record player	rekoodo-pureeyaa
radio	rajio
cassette	kasetto
cassette tape	kasetto-teepu

radio & cassette player	raji-kase
tape recorder	teepu-rekoodaa
cassette tape recorder	kasetto-teepu-rekoodaa
television	terebi
video recorder	bideo, VTR
video tape	bideo-teepu
LD, laser disk	reezaa-disuku
laser disk player	reezaa-disuku-pureeyaa
CD, compact disk	shiidii
CD player	shiidii-pureeyaa
amplifier	anpu
microphone	maiku
headset, earphones	heddohon
speaker	supiikaa
adaptor	adaputaa
micro computer	maikon
personal computer	pasokon
family computer	famikon
TV game	terebi-geemu

electronic calculator	dentaku
toaster	toosutaa
microwave oven	denshirenji
refrigerator	reezooko
food mixer	mikisaa
food processor	fuudo-purosessaa
rice cooker	suihanki
electric washer	sentakuki
iron	airon
hair dryer	doraiyaa
electric fan	senpuuki
table with heating unit	kotatsu
plug	puragu
facsimile	fakushimiri
telex	terekkusu
photocopy	kopii
height	takasa
weight	omosa
depth, length	okuyuki
width	haba

Cameras, watches, photography

photograph	shashin
camera	kamera
enlargement	hikinobashi
developing	genzoo
print	yakitsuke, purinto
additional copy	yakimashi
film	fuirumu
8mm film	hachimiri-fuirumu
black and white	shirokuro (fuirumu)
color	karaa (fuirumu)
thirty-six exposure film	36(sanjuuroku)-mai-dori-no fuirumu
lens	renzu
shutter	shattaa
flash	furasshu
light meter	roshutsukee
filter	firutaa
slide	suraido
video camera	bideo-kamera
watch	tokee
wall clock	kakedokee

table clock	okidokee
alarm clock	mezamashidokee
wrist watch	udedokee
game watch	geemuuotchi
battery	kan-denchi, denchi

Cosmetics

cosmetics	keshoohin
lipstick	kuchibeni
face powder	oshiroi
cream	kuriim
lotion	keshoosui
eye liner	ai-rainaa
nail polish	manikyua
nail polish remover	manikyua-rimuubaa
perfume	koosui
blush	hoobeni
eau de Cologne	oodekoron
setting lotion	setto-rooshon
foundation	fandeeshon
hand cream	hando-kuriim
sun-tan oil [cream]	hiyakedome

comb	kushi
hairbrush	burashi
sponge	suponji
compact	konpakuto
hairpin	heapin
wig	katsura
shampoo	shanpuu
treatment cream	toriitomento-kuriimu
rinse	rinsu
soap	sekken
razor	kamisori
razor blades	kamisori-no ha
after-shave lotion	afutaa-sheebu-rooshon
shaving cream	sheebingu-kuriim
toothpaste	hamigaki
toothbrush	haburashi
nail clippers	tsumekiri

Stationery, books

pencil	enpitsu
eraser	keshigomu
pen	pen

fountain pen	mannenhitsu
ink	inku
ball-point pen	booru-pen
mechanical pencil	shaapu-pensiru
felt-tipped pen	sainpen
notebook	nooto
envelope	fuutoo
letter pad	binsen
picture postcard	e-hagaki
file	fairu
ruler, square	joogi
pencil sharpener	enpitsu-kezuri
paste, glue	nori
string	himo
book	hon
book in Japanese	nihongo-no hon
book in English	eego-no hon
nonfiction	nonfikushon
novel	shoosetsu
foreign book	yoosho
dictionary	jisho
English-Japanese	eewa-jiten

dictionary	
Japanese-English dictionary	waee-jiten
encyclopedia	hyakka-jiten
magazine	zasshi
monthly magazine	gekkanshi
weekly magazine	shuukanshi
newspaper	shinbun
newspaper in Japanese	nihongo-no shinbun
newspaper in English	eeji-shinbun
map	chizu

Daily necessities

towel	taoru
tissues	tisshu-peepaa
toilet paper	toiretto-peepaa
curtain	kaaten
clothespin	sentakubasami
pillow	makura
pillow case	makura-kabaa

sheet	shiitsu
bedding, mattress, quilt	futon
blanket	moofu
detergent	senzai
sanitary napkin	seeriyoohin
rug	shikimono

Vehicles

bicycle	jitensha
motorbike	ootobai
car	kuruma, jidoosha
secondhand	chuuko

INFORMATION

★ You can make a call without coins using a telephone card.

★ There are some phones from which you can make international calls in large metropolitan areas.

★ For information :
Dial 104 (local)
Dial 105 (long-distance)

★ For international calls through an operator :
Dial 0051 for KDD (Kokusai Denpou Denwakyoku).

5. Road and Traffic

Asking for directions

1. I'm lost.

   Michi-ni mayoimashita.

2. Could you draw me a map, please?

   Chizu-o kaite-itadake-masu-ka.

3. Where am I now on this map?

   Kono-chizu-dewa genzaichi-wa doko-ni narimasu-ka.

4. Will you tell me how to get to American Embassy?

   Amerika-taishikan-made donoyoo-ni iku-no-ka oshiete-kuremasu-ka.

5. How do I get to ～station?

   ～eki-wa donoyoo-ni ittara ii-desu-ka.

6. Is there a subway station around here?

   Kono-chikaku-ni chikatetsu-no eki-wa arimasu-ka.

7. Which way is it to the museum in Ueno?

   Ueno-no hakubutsukan-wa dochira-no michi-desu-ka.

8. Is it near the station?

   Eki-ni chikai-desu-ka.

9. How far is it? — Dono-kurai-no kyori desu-ka.

10. How long will it take on foot? — Aruite dono-kurai kakarimasu-ka.

11. How far is it from Hibiya station? — Hibiya-eki-kara dono-kurai-no kyori desu-ka.

Traffic

1. I'll take a subway [bus/taxi/train]. — Chikatetsu [basu/taku-shii/densha]-ni norimasu.

2. Does this bus [train] stop at ～? — Kono basu [densha]-wa ～-ni tomarimasu-ka.

3. How many stops are there? — Eki-wa ikutsu arimasu-ka.

4. What is the best way to go to Yokohama? — Yokohama-e iku-ni-wa dono kootsuukikan-ga ichi-ban ii-desu-ka.

5. Which is better, to — Basu-to takushii-dewa

go by bus or by taxi?   dochira-de iku-no-ga ii-
                          desu-ka.

Subway, railroad

1. Which line do I   Nani-sen-ni noreba
   take?   ii-desu-ka.

2. What track does   Nan-bansen kara
   the train leave from?   demasu-ka.

3. Does this go to Asa-   Kore-wa Asakusa-iki
   kusa?   desu-ka.

4. Is this the right   Hachiooji-iki-no
   platform for Hachi-   purattohoomu-wa   koko
   ooji?   desu-ka.

5. What time will we   Nanji-ni Ueno-ni tsuki-
   arrive at Ueno?   masu-ka.

6. How long will it   Chikatetsu-desu-to,
   take to go to Aki-   Akihabara-made dono-
   habara by subway?   kurai jikan-ga
                       kakarimasu-ka.

7. What time is the   Tsugi-no Oosaka-iki-wa

next train for Osaka?	nan-ji-ni demasu-ka.
8. What time does the super express train for Hakata leave?	Hakata-iki-no shinkansen-wa nan-ji-ni demasu-ka.
9. What time does the last train leave?	Shuuden-wa nan-ji-ni demasu-ka.
10. May I have a subway route map?	Chikatetsu-rosenzu-o itadakemasu-ka.

Buying tickets

1. Where's the ticket office?	Kippu-uriba-wa doko desu-ka.
2. Where can I buy a book of subway tickets [commuter pass]?	Chikatetsu-no kaisuuken [teeki]-wa doko-de kaemasu-ka.
3. Will you show me how to use this vending machine?	Kono jidoohanbaiki-no tsukaikata-o oshiete-moraemasu-ka.
4. What is the fare to	~-made ikura desu-ka.

~ ?

5. What's the one-way [round trip] fare ?

Katamichi-ryookin [Oofuku-ryookin]-wa ikura desu-ka.

6. What's the express charge ?

Kyuukoo-ryookin-wa ikura desu-ka.

7. Is the express charge included ?

Kyuukoo-ryookin-wa fukumarete-imasu-ka.

8. I would like to buy a reserved seat for the 10 o'clock super express Hikari for tomorrow morning.

Asu-no gozen juuji-no hikari-goo-no shiteeseki-o kaitai-no-desu.

Trains

1. Is this seat taken ?

Kono seki-wa fusagatte-imasu-ka.

2. Excuse me, could you move over a little, please ?

Sumimasen-ga, sukoshi seki-o tsumete-itadake-masu-ka.

3. Do you mind if I smoke?

Tabako-o sutte-mo kamaimasen-ka.

4. I'd like to move to the no-smoking area if there's room.

Kuuseki-ga areba kin'enseki-ni utsuritai-no-desu.

5. Where's the lavatory?

Keshooshitsu-wa doko desu-ka.

6. Is there any conductor who speaks English?

Eego-no wakaru shashoo-san-wa imasu-ka.

Transfering

1. Will you tell me where to change trains?

Doko-de norikaeru-no-ka oshiete-moraemasu-ka.

2. It's the one after next.

Tsugi-no tsugi desu.

3. Where should I change trains to go to Narita?

Densha-de Narita-e iku-niwa doko-de norikaeru-no-desu-ka.

Asking about destinations

1. What is the next station[stop]?
   Tsugi-no eki-wa doko desu-ka.

2. Which stop should I get off at?
   Dono eki-de oriru-no-desu-ka.

3. Is the next stop Ginza?
   Tsugi-wa Ginza desu-ka.

4. How many stops is that from here?
   Koko-kara ikutsume desu-ka.

Buses／Asking about bus stops

1. Where can I get a bus?
   Doko-de basu-ni noru-koto-ga dekimasu-ka.

2. Is this the bus stop for Shinjuku?
   Koko-wa Shinjuku-iki-no basutee desu-ka.

Asking about destinations

1. Does this bus go to Shibuya?
   Kono basu-wa Shibuya-e ikimasu-ka.

2. Which bus goes to Shinjuku?

Dono basu-ga Shinjuku-e ikimasu-ka.

3. What's the number of the bus that goes to Tsukuba?

Tsukuba-e iku basu-wa nan-ban-ka oshiete-itadake-masu-ka.

4. It is a No. 18 bus.

Juuhachi-ban-no basu desu.

5. Does this bus stop at Harajuku?

Kono basu-wa Harajuku-ni tomarimasu-ka.

Time and distance

1. What time does the next bus come?

Tsugi-no basu-wa nan-ji-ni kimasu-ka.

2. What time is the last bus?

Saishuu-basu-no jikan-wa nan-ji desu-ka.

3. Is the airport bus coming soon?

Kuukoo-basu-wa sugu-ni kimasu-ka.

4. How long will it take by bus?

Basu-desu-to dono-kurai-no jikan-ga

kakarimasu-ka.

Fares

1. How much is the fare to City Hall?

   Shiyakusho-made ikura desu-ka.

2. Do I pay before or after?

   Maebarai desu-ka atobarai desu-ka.

3. Please give me a book of tickets for the bus.

   Basu-no kaisuuken-o kudasai.

4. Can you change a one thousand yen bill?

   Sen-en-satsu-wa ryoogae dekimasu-ka.

Getting off a bus

1. Which stop should I get off at?

   Dono teeryuujo-de oriru-no-desu-ka.

2. I'm getting off.

   Orimasu.

Miscellaneous

1. May I smoke on the bus?

Basu-no naka-de tabako-o sutte-mo ii-desu-ka.

2. Where are we now?

Ima doko-o hashitte-imasu-ka.

3. Where can I buy a bus commutation pass?

Basu-no teeki-wa doko-de kaemasu-ka.

Taxis/Taxi stands

1. Where's the taxi stand?

Takushii-noriba-wa doko desu-ka.

2. I'd like you to call a taxi, please.

Takushii-o yonde-itadakitai-no-desu.

Fares

1. How much will it cost to get to Ikebukuro by taxi?

Takushii-de Ikebukuro-made ikura desu-ka.

2. Can you take me to Tokyo Disneyland for under two thousand yen?

Nisen-en-inai-de Tookyoo-dizunii-rando-e ikemasu-ka.

Asking about destinations

1. May I get in? — Notte-mo ii-desu-ka.

2. Where would you like to go? — Dochira-e.

3. Take me to the Akasaka Prince Hotel, please. — Akasaka-Purinsu-Hoteru-made itte-kudasai.

4. Take me to this address, please. — Kono juusho-no tokoro-e itte-kudasai.

5. Please go quickly. — Isoide kudasai.

6. Please turn right [left] at the next corner. — Tsugi-no kado-o migi [hidari]-ni magatte-kudasai.

Getting out of a taxi

1. Stop here, please.   Koko-de tomete-kudasai.

2. Let me off at the next corner, please.   Tsugi-no kado-de oroshite-kudasai.

3. Please wait here for a minute.   Koko-de sukoshi matteite-kudasai.

4. Keep the change.   Otsuri-wa irimasen.

Airplanes／Tickets, reservations

1. I'd like to reconfirm my flight from Tokyo to Paris.   Tookyoo-kara Pari-made-no bin-no yoyaku-o saikakunin-shitai-no-desu.

2. I'd like to change my reservation.   Yoyaku-no henkoo-o onegai-shitai-no-desu.

3. Which counter should I go to?   Dono kauntaa-ni ikeba ii-desu-ka.

On the plane

1. May I have some-
thing to read ?

Nani-ka yomumono-o
itadake-masu-ka.

2. Can I get some
aspirin ?

Asupirin-o itadake-
masu-ka.

3. When will we land
in Nagasaki ?

Itsu Nagasaki-ni tsuki-
masu-ka.

4. Are we arriving on
time ?

Teekoku-no toochaku
desu-ka.

Baggage

1. Where can I pick up
my baggage ?

Doko-de nimotsu-o
uketoru-no-desu-ka.

2. I can't find my
bags.

Nimotsu-ga miatari-
masen.

3. Will you carry my
bags ?

Nimotsu-o hakon-de
moraemasu-ka.

Cars／Rent-a-car

1. I'd like to rent a

Kuruma-o karitai-nocar.

desu.

2. This is my International Driver's Licence.

Kore-ga watashi-no kokusai-untenmenkyo-shoo desu.

3. How much is the rate?

Ryookin-wa ikura desu-ka.

4. Does that include gas?

Gasorin-dai-wa komi desu-ka.

5. Do you require a deposit?

Hoshookin-ga hitsuyoo desu-ka.

6. What kind of cars do you have?

Donna kuruma-ga arimasu-ka.

7. I'd like to take out an insurance policy.

Hoken-o kaketai-no-desu.

8. I'd like to leave it in Hiroshima.

Hiroshima-ni norisutetai-no-desu.

Gas stations

1. Where's the nearest gas station?

Ichiban-chikai gasorin-sutando-wa doko desu-

ka.

2. My car is out of gas.

Gasorin-ga nakunari-mashita.

3. How much is it per liter?

Ichi-rittaa ikura desu-ka.

4. Please fill it up.

Mantan-ni shite-kudasai.

5. This car isn't in good condition.

Kuruma-no chooshi-ga warui-no-desu.

6. Will you check the car thoroughly?

Sumi-kara sumi-made tenkenshite-itadakemasu-ka.

7. I've got a flat.

Panku-shite-shimai-mashita.

Driving

1. What's the speed limit here?

Koko-no seegen-sokudo-wa dono-kurai desu-ka.

2. Is this a one-way street?

Ippoo-tsuukoo desu-ka.

3. Where can I park around here?

Kono-hen-de chuusha dekiru-no-wa doko desu-ka.

Travel miscellaneous

1. What exit is this?

Nani-guchi desu-ka.

2. How do you get to the south exit?

Minami-guchi-wa donoyoo-ni ikimasu-ka.

3. I missed the train.

Densha-ni noriokure-mashita.

4. I bought the wrong ticket.

Machigatta kippu-o katte-shimai-mashita.

5. I lost my ticket.

Kippu-o nakushi-mashita.

6. Where can I get this ticket refunded?

Doko-de kono kippu-o haraimodosukoto-ga dekimasu-ka.

7. Do you have a time-table?

Jikokuhyoo-ga arimasu-ka.

Traffic

ticket	kippu (densha, chikatetsu, *etc.*)
map	chizu
guide book	annaisho, gaido bukku
ship	fune
car ferry	kaa ferii
police box	kooban
traffic light	shingoo
pedestrian over- pass	hodookyoo
pedestrian crossing	oodan-hodoo
intersection	koosaten
~ street	~ doori
(go) straight	massugu (ni-iku)
(go) right	migi (e-iku)
(go) left	hidari (e-iku)
traffic jam	juutai
rush hour	rasshu-awaa
pedestrian street	hokoosha-tengoku
destination	mokutekichi

Subway, railroad

station	eki
station attendant	eki'in
conductor	shashoo
ticket window	kippu-uriba
ticket vending machine	jidoo-kenbaiki
Special Ticket Window	Midori-no madoguchi
adult	otona
child	kodomo
limited express ticket	tokkyuuken
green car ticket, first class seat ticket	guriinken
round trip ticket	oofukukippu
one-way ticket	katamichikippu
sightseeing ticket	syuuyuuken
limited sightseeing ticket	mini-syuuyuuken
JR (Japanese	jeeaaru

Railways)

electric train	densha
subway	chikatetsu
platform	noriba
platform	hoomu
track three	sanbansen
entrance	iriguchi
exit	deguchi
north entrance	kitaguchi
south entrance	minamiguchi
west entrance	nishiguchi
east entrance	higashiguchi
wicket	kaisatsuguchi
local train	kakuekiteesha
express train	kyuukoo
rapid-service train	kaisoku-densha
special rapid service train	tokubetsu-kaisoku-densha
no-smoking car	kin'ensha
sleeping car	shindaisha
dining car	shokudoosha
front car	ichiban mae-no kuruma

front car	sentoo-no kuruma
last car	ichiban ushiro-no kuruma
car No. 5	go-goosha
non-reserved seat	jiyuuseki
reserved seat	shiteeseki
train schedule	jikokuhyoo
subway map	chikatetsu-rosenzu
Lost & Found	wasuremono toriatsukaijo
fare adjustment window	seesanjo
tourist information office	annaijo
information	annaijo
kiosk	baiten, kiosuku
emergency service office	ryokoosha-engojo
coin-operated locker	koin-rokkaa
left luggage	nimotsu-ichiji-azukarijo
ticket check	kensatsu
arrival	toochaku
departure	hassha, shuppatsu

| transfer, change | norikae |
| redcap | akaboo |

Buses

bus	basu
tariff	ryookinhyoo
bus stop	basutee
highway express bus	haiuee basu

Cars

road map	dooro-chizu
parking lot	chuusha-joo
gas station	gasorin-sutando
gas	gasorin
oil	oiru
flat	panku
tire	taiya
steering wheel	handoru
brake	bureeki
horn	kurakushon
rearview mirror	bakku-miraa

windshield	**furonto-garasu**

Airplanes

airplane	**hikooki**
airport	**kuukoo**
boarding pass	**toojooken**
take-off	**ririku**
landing	**chakuriku**
claim tag	**nimotsu-uketorishoo**
occupied	**shiyoochuu**

Special Ticket Window

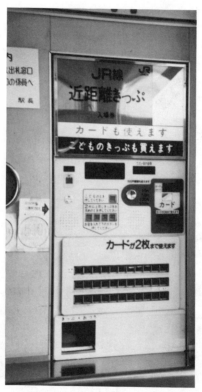

Ticket Vending Machine

6. Entertainment

Tickets, information

1. Where's a theater ticket agency?

   Pureegaido-wa doko desu-ka.

2. I'd like information for plays and concerts.

   Engeki-to konsaato-no annai-ga hoshii-no-desu.

3. Could you sell me a ticket for the opera?

   Opera-no kippu-o onegai-dekimasu-ka.

4. Where's the ticket office?

   Kippu-uriba-wa doko desu-ka.

5. Are there any seats left?

   Mada seki-wa arimasu-ka.

6. What kind of seats are available?

   Donna seki-ga arimasu-ka.

7. How much are the tickets?

   Nyuujooryoo-wa ikura-desu-ka.

8. How much are general admission seats?

   Ippanseki-wa ikura desu-ka.

9. How much are reserved seats?

   Shiteeseki-wa ikura-desu-ka.

10. How much are the least expensive seats? — Ichiban yasui-no-wa ikura desu-ka.

11. One general admission seat, please. — Ippanseki-o ichimai kudasai.

12. Two reserved seats for tonight, please. — Kon'ya-no shiteeseki-o nimai kudasai.

13. Do I have to book tickets in advance? — Maeuri-o katteokanakute-wa-narimasen-ka.

14. I'm looking for seat number 12, in row E. — Ii-retsu juuniban-no seki-o sagashite-imasu.

Movies

1. What films are showing now? — Ima donna eega-ga jooee-sarete-imasu-ka.

2. Where is this movie showing? — Sono eega-wa doko-de jooee-sarete-imasu-ka.

3. Until what date is this movie showing? — Kono eega-wa itsu-made jooee-saremasu-ka.

4. What time does the movie start ?

Eega-wa nan-ji-ni hajimarimasu-ka.

5. What time does the last feature begin ?

Saishuukai-wa nan-ji-kara desu-ka.

6. What kind of film is it ?

Donna eega desu-ka.

7. Is it a comedy ?

Sore-wa kigeki desu-ka.

8. Is it suitable for children ?

Sore-wa kodomo-ni-mo miseraremasu-ka.

9. Is this movie dubbed or subtitled ?

Fukikae desu-ka,soretomo jimaku-ga demasu-ka.

10. Who's the star ?

Shuyaku-wa dare desu-ka.

Theater

1. What's showing at the National Theater ?

Kokuritsu-gekijoo-dewa nani-o jooen-shite-imasu-ka.

2. What kind of play is it ?

Sore-wa donna geki desu-ka.

3. What kind of story is it?

Sore-wa donna suji desu-ka.

4. Does the cast of the play include famous actors?

Sono geki-niwa yuumee-na haiyuu-ga shutsuen-shite-imasu-ka.

5. When's the last day of the performance?

Senshuuraku-wa itsu desu-ka.

Music

1. I'd like to go to a concert tonight.

Kon'ya konsaato-ni ikitai-no-desu.

2. Who's the conductor?

Shikisha-wa dare desu-ka.

3. Who is performing?

Sono konsaato-dewa dare-ga ensoo-shimasu-ka.

Sports

1. I'd like to play tennis.

Tenisu-ga shitai-no-desu.

2. I want to go swimming.

Oyogi-ni ikitai-desu.

3. I'd like to watch *sumo* wrestling.

Sumoo-ga mitai-no-desu.

4. I'd like to watch a baseball game.

Yakyuu-no-shiai-ga mitai-no-desu.

5. What's the most popular sport here?

Koko-de ichiban ninki-no-aru-supootsu-wa nan desu-ka.

6. Can we rent a court?

Kooto-o karirukoto-ga dekimasu-ka.

7. What kind of facilities are available now?

Ima donna shisetsu-ga riyoo dekimasu-ka.

8. Who's the opposing team?

Taisen'aite-wa doko desu-ka.

9. I don't understand the rules well.

Ruuru-ga yoku wakaranai-no-desu.

10. Could you explain the rules?

Ruuru-o setsumee-shite-itadakemasu-ka.

168

Television

1. I'd rather watch TV in my room.

   Watashi-wa heya-de terebi-o miteiru-hoo-ga ii-desu.

2. What channel is the baseball game on?

   Yakyuu-no shiai-wa nan-channeru desu-ka.

3. Is this broadcast bilingual?

   Kore-wa nikakokugo-hoosoo desu-ka.

4. Is there a television guide written in English?

   Eego-no terebi-annai-wa arimasu-ka.

Other entertainment

1. I'd like to go disco-dancing.

   Disuko-e odori-ni ikitai-no-desu.

2. What's the most famous disco in Roppongi?

   Roppongi-de ichiban yuumee-na disuko-wa doko desu-ka.

3. Where would you suggest I go for a

   Ippai nomu-niwa donna tokoro-ga ii-deshoo-ka.

drink ?

4. I'd like to see a local folk dance.

Kono chihoo-no minzoku-buyoo-ga mitai-no-desu.

Miscellaneous

1. How should I dress ?

Donoyoo-na fukusoo-o shiteikeba ii-deshoo-ka.

2. Will I need opera glasses from that seat ?

Sono seki-kara-dato opera-gurasu-ga irimasu-ka.

3. What time should I leave the hotel to be in time for the play ?

Oshibai-ni maniau-tame-niwa nan-ji-ni hoteru-o dere-ba yoroshii-desu-ka.

4. I'm too tired to go out.

Tsukarete gaishutsu-suru-ki-ga shimasen.

Entertainment

movie	eega
theater (movie)	eegakan
play, drama, performance	engeki
theater (play)	gekijoo
subtitles	jimaku
actor	haiyuu
actress	joyuu
director	kantoku
new film	shinsakueega
science fiction	esuefu
war film	sensooeega
love story	ren'aimono
crime story	hanzaimono
mystery	suirimono
horror film	kyoofueega
western	seebugeki
adventure story	bookenmono
now showing (film)	jooeechuu

now playing (theater)	jooen-chuu
adult	otona
child	kodomo
student	gakusee
ticket for today	toojitsuken
advance booking	maeuriken
unreserved seat	jiyuuseki
reserved seat	shiteeseki
standing room	tachimi

7. Sightseeing

Package tours

1. Where is the J. T. B
   office ?

   Kootsuu-koosha-wa
   doko desu-ka.

2. Could you tell me
   the way to the tourist
   information office,
   please ?

   Kankoo-annaijo-e iku
   michi-o oshiete-
   itadakemasu-ka.

3. What kind of tours
   do you have ?

   Donna tsuaa-ga
   arimasu-ka.

4. May I have a bro-
   chure ?

   Panfuretto-o
   itadakemasu-ka.

5. Could you suggest
   any interesting places
   to visit in Kamaku-
   ra ?

   Kamakura-no meesho-o
   shookai-shite-itadake-
   masu-ka.

6. Do you have a tour
   that goes to Mt.
   Fuji ?

   Fujisan-e iku tsuaa-wa
   arimasu-ka.

7. Is it possible to rent
   a country house for a

   Ni-san-nichi bessoo-o
   karirukoto-ga dekimasu-

few days ?
ka.

8. I'd like to join a tour.
Tsuaa-ni sanka-shitai-no-desu.

9. Can I join the tour en route ?
Tochuu-kara sanka dekimasu-ka.

10. Can we have an English-speaking guide ?
Eego-o hanasu gaido-o tsukete-moraemasu-ka.

Tour's contents

1. Is it a full day tour ?
Higaeri-tsuaa desu-ka.

2. Could you tell me the schedule in detail ?
Yotee-o kuwashiku oshiete-itadakemasu-ka.

3. Where does it begin ?
Shuppatsu-wa doko-kara desu-ka.

4. What time does it start ?
Shuppatsu-wa nan-ji desu-ka.

5. How long is this tour ?
Sono tsuaa-wa dono-kurai jikan-ga

175

	kakarimasu-ka.
6. One week.	Isshuukan desu.
7. What's the price of the tour?	Tsuaa-no ryookin-wa ikura desu-ka.
8. What's included in this price?	Kono ryookin-niwa nani-ga fukumarete-imasu-ka.
9. Are meals included?	Shokujidai-wa haitte-imasu-ka.
10. Are all tranportation costs included?	Kootsuuhi-wa zenbu komi desu-ka.
11. Will I need ∼?	∼-wa hitsuyoo desu-ka.

Touring

1. What is scheduled for today?	Kyoo-wa nani-o yatte-imasu-ka.
2. Can I go into this building?	Tatemono-no naka-ni hairemasu-ka.
3. Does it cost any-	Tatemono-no naka-ni

thing to enter this building?	hairu-nowa yuuryoo desu-ka.
4. Where can I register for a tour?	Doko-de kengaku-o mooshikomukoto-ga dekimasu-ka.
5. Is it famous historically?	Rekishiteki-ni yuumee desu-ka.
6. What's it famous for?	Nani-de yuumee desu-ka.
7. What festival is that?	Are-wa nanno omatsuri desu-ka.
8. What ceremony is that?	Are-wa nanno gishiki desu-ka.
9. May I take a picture of this?	Kono shashin-o totte-mo kamaimasen-ka.
10. May I take pictures inside the museum?	Bijutsukan-no naka-de shashin-o totte-mo ii-desu-ka.
11. Excuse me, could I	Shitsurei-desu-ga,

take a picture with you, please?

issho-ni shashin-o torasete-itadakemasu-ka.

12. Excuse me, may I take your picture, please?

Shitsuree-desu-ga, shashin-o torasete-itadakemasu-ka.

13. Do you know if there are any toilets around here?

Kono atari-ni toire-ga aru-ka doo-ka gozonji desu-ka.

14. Is this place off limits?

Koko-wa tachiiri-kinshi desu-ka.

15. How was the trip to Kyoto?

Kyooto-ryokoo-wa ikaga deshita-ka.

Traditional performing arts

1. Where can I see a Kabuki performance [a Noh play, a Bunraku puppet show, sumo wrestling]?

Kabuki [Noo, Bunraku, Sumoo]-wa doko-de miraremasu-ka.

2. What is showing now?

Ima nani-o yatte-imasu-ka.

3. How long will it run?

Nan-nichi-made yatte-imasu-ka.

4. Do you have an English pamphlet?

Eebun-no panfuretto-wa arimasuka.

5. Can I rent an English earphone?

Eego-no iyahon-wa kariraremasu-ka.

6. I would like to try to make pottery.

Toogee-o yattemitai-no-desu.

7. I would like to try to wear a kimono.

Kimono-o kitemitai-no-desu.

Sightseeing

sightseeing	kankoo
Japan Travel Bureau, J. T. B.	kootsuu-koosha
Tourist Information Center	kankoo-annaijo
travel agent	kankoo-ryokoosha
guide-book	ryokoo-annaisho
sightseeing bus	kankoo basu
tour guide	kankoo gaido
entrance fee	nyuujooryoo
lost and found	ishitsubutsu-toriatsukaijo

Tourist facilities

famous spot	meesho
place of historical interest	kyuuseki
ruins	iseki
monument	ki'nenhi
castle	shiro
shrine	jinja
temple	otera, tera

church	kyookai
garden	niwa
ceremony	gishiki
museum	hakubutsukan
art museum	bijutsukan
botanical garden	shokubutsuen
amusement park	yuuenchi
zoo	doobutsuen
aquarium	suizokukan
stadium	sutajiamu
market	ichiba
sea	umi
seashore, beach	kaigan
mountain	yama
river	kawa
lake	mizuumi
water fall	taki
hot spring	onsen
bridge	hashi
harbor	minato
water fountain	funsui
fishing	tsuri

181

mountain-climbing	yamanobori
music	ongaku
folk music	minzokuongaku
classical music	koten'ongaku

À la Japanese

tea ceremony	sadoo
powdered tea used for tea ceremony	matcha
flower arrangement	ikebana
Kabuki performance	kabuki
Noh play	noo
Bunraku puppet show	bunraku
offering	osaisen
written oracle	omikuji
charm, amulet	omamori
fire works	hanabi
festival	matsuri

Japanese classical dance	Nihonbuyoo

"Forbidden"

danger	kiken
no admittance	tachiirikinshi
no smoking	kin'en
forbidden to take photos	satsueekinshi
tripods forbidden	sankyaku-shiyookinshi
flash forbidden	furasshu-no shiyookinshi
high voltage	kooatsu
out of order	koshoo
caution	chuui
stop	tomare
under construction	kooji-chuu
no parking	chuushakinshi
Please don't litter.	Gomi-o sutenaide-kudasai.
Please keep off the grass.	Shibafu-no naka-ni hairanaide-kudasai.
Do not touch.	Te-o furenaide-kudasai.

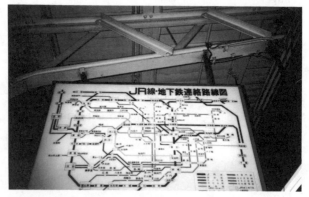

Route Map (JR and subway)

8. Telephone

Looking for a phone

1. I'd like to make a phone call.

   Denwa-ga kaketai-no-desu.

2. Where can I find a pay phone?

   Kooshuu-denwa-wa doko desu-ka.

3. May I use your phone, please?

   Denwa-o okari-dekimasu-ka.

4. Could you tell me how to make a call from this phone, please?

   Kono-denwa-no kakekata-o oshiete-itadakemasu-ka.

Making a phone call

1. Hello.

   Moshi, moshi.

2. Just a moment, please.

   Shooshoo omachi-kudasai.

3. Hold the line, please.

   Sonomama-de omachi-kudasai.

4. I can't get through on this phone.

   Denwa-ga tsunagari-masen.

5. The line is busy.　　Hanashi-chuu-desu.

6. I can't hear you.　　Kikoenai-no-desu-ga.

7. Would you please repeat that?　　Moo-ichido itte-itadake-masu-ka.

8. Please speak more slowly.　　Moo-sukoshi yukkuri itte-kudasai.

9. Could you speak louder, please?　　Motto ookii-koe-de hanashite-itadakemasu-ka.

10. Please speak in English.　　Eego-de onegai-shimasu.

11. I don't have any more coins.　　Moo kozeni-ga arimasen.

Getting your party on the line

1. Hello, is this Mr. Tanaka?　　Moshi moshi, Tanaka-san desu-ka.

2. Is this Mr. Takeda's residence?　　Takeda-san-no otaku desu-ka.

3. This is Smith　　Sumisu-to mooshimasu.

speaking.

4. Is Mr. Matsushita in?	Matsushita-san-wa irasshaimasu-ka.
5. May I speak to Mr. Ozawa?	Ozawa-san-o onegai-shimasu.
6. Extension 257, please.	Naisen ni-go-nana-ban-o onegai-shimasu.
7. Make it a person-to-person call, please.	Shimee-tsuuwa-ni shite-kudasai.
8. Make it a collect call, please.	Korekuto-kooru-ni shite-kudasai.

Answering the telephone

1. Who is speaking, please?	Dochira-sama deshoo-ka.
2. He[She] is out at the moment.	Ima gaishutsu-chuu desu.
3. No, you have the wrong number.	Iie, chigaimasu.

Ending a conversation

1. I'll call you back right away.

Sugu kakenaoshimasu.

2. I'll call again.

Mata denwa-shimasu.

3. What time shall I call you back?

Nan-ji-ni odenwa-shimashoo-ka.

4. Please call me.

Denwa-shite-kudasai.

5. Would you mind calling back later?

Nochihodo odenwa-o itadakemasu-ka.

6. Thank you for your call.

Odenwa arigatoo-gozaimashita.

Leaving a message

1. May I leave a message?

Dengon-o onegai-dekimasu-ka.

2. Could you please tell Mr. Sakamoto that I called?

Sakamoto-san-ni denwa-ga attakoto-o otsutae-itadakemasu-ka.

Requesting a phone number

1. Please tell me your phone number.

Anata-no denwa-bangoo-o oshiete-kudasai.

2. What number is information?

Bangoo-annai-wa nan-ban desu-ka.

3. I'd like the number of the Holiday Inn.

Horidee-In-no bangoo-o oshiete-itadakitai-no-desu.

4. What is the area code for Chiba city?

Chibashi-no shigai-kyokuban-wa ikutsu desu-ka.

International calls

1. I'd like to make an international phone call.

Kokusai-denwa-ga kaketai-no-desu.

2. Can I make international calls from this public telephone?

Kono-kooshuu-denwa-de kokusai-denwa-ga kakeraremasu-ka.

3. I'd like to get International Telephone Call Service.

Kokusai-tsuuwa-no kookan-ga yobitai-no-desu.

4. I'd like to make a call to New York.

Nyuuyooku-ni denwa-ga-shitai-no-desu.

5. Can I call India directly from here?

Koko-kara Indo-ni chokutsuu-denwa-ga kakeraremasu-ka.

6. Can I make a collect call to Hong-Kong?

Honkon-e korekuto-kooru-ga kakeraremasu-ka.

7. I'd like to make a person-to-person international call.

Kokusai-shimee-tsuuwa-o onegai-shimasu.

8. What's the international phone code for Canada?

Kanada-no kokusai-denwa-no kyoku-bangoo-wa nan-ban desu-ka.

9. Could you cancel my call to London?

Rondon-eno tsuuwa-o torikeshite-kudasai.

10. What time is it now in Rome?   Rooma-dewa ima nan-ji-desu-ka.

11. Let me know the charge later, please.   Atode ryookin-o shirasete-kudasai.

Miscellaneous

1. I'd like to buy a telephone card.   Terehon-kaado-ga kaitai-no-desu.

2. Please change this into 10 yen coins.   Kore-o juuen-dama-ni kaete-kudasai.

INFORMATION

In case of emergency:
    Dial 110 (Police)
    Dial 119 (Fire and Ambulance)

Telephone

telephone	denwa
telephone box, telephone booth	denwa-bokkusu
public telephone	kooshuu-denwa
telephone book	denwachoo
telephone office	denwakyoku
telephone number	denwa-bango
extension	naisen
operator	opereetaa
message	dengon
direct call	dairekuto-kooru
collect call	korekuto-kooru
person-to-person call	paasonaru-kooru
local call	shinai-tsuuwa
long distance call	shigai-tsuuwa
overseas call	kokusai-denwa
telephone card	terehon-kaado

International Telephone Box

9. Mail

Mail

1. Where's the post office?

Yuubinkyoku-wa doko-desu-ka.

2. Is there a mailbox around here?

Kono atari-ni posuto-ga arimasu-ka.

3. Where can I get postcards and envelopes?

Hagaki-to fuutoo-wa doko-de kaemasu-ka.

4. At which window do they sell stamps?

Kitte-wa dono mado-guchi-desu-ka.

5. Please give me three 170 yen stamps.

170 (Hyaku-nanajuu)-en -no kitte-o sanmai kudasai.

6. Which slot should I put overseas mail in?

Gaikoku-yuubin-wa dochira desu-ka.

7. Please show me the list of zip codes.

Yuubin-bangoo-bo-o misete-kudasai.

8. Please tell me the postal code [zip code] for Meguro ward.

Meguro-ku-no yuubin-bangoo-o oshiete-kudasai.

Postal charges, etc.

1. How much is the postage?

Yuubin-ryookin-wa ikura desu-ka.

2. How much will it be by airmail [seamail]?

Kookuubin [Funabin]-desu-to ikura kakarimasu-ka.

3. How much is the postage to Brazil?

Burajiru-made ikura-desu-ka.

4. How long does it take to Thailand?

Tai-made dono kurai kakarimasu-ka.

Express, registered mail

1. By express mail, please.

Sokutatsu-de onegai-shimasu.

2. By registered mail, please.

Kakitome-de onegai-shimasu.

Parcel post, packages

1. Please send this parcel.

Kono kozutsumi-o onegai-shimasu.

2. Could you weigh this package ?

Kono kozutsumi-no omosa-o hakatte-itadakemasu-ka.

3. I'd like to send this parcel to Washington.

Kono kozutsumi-o washinton-e okuritai-no-desu.

4. May I enclose a letter in it ?

Tegami-o doofuu-shite-mo ii-desu-ka.

Mail

post office	yuubinkyoku
mailbox	posuto
counter, window	madoguchi
(Window No.1)	(ichiban madoguchi)
post card	hagaki
picture post card	e-hagaki
letter	tegami
aerogram	earoguramu, kookuushokan
parcel, package	kozutsumi
address	atesaki, banchi, juusho
name	namae
zip code, postal code	yuubin-bangoo
postage	yuubin-ryookin
postage stamp	kitte
sixty-yen stamp	rokujuu-en kitte
forty-yen stamp	yonjuu-en-kitte
airmail	kookuubin
seamail	funabin
registered	kakitome
express, special delivery	sokutatsu

mail carrier	yuubin-haitatsu
telegram	denpoo
international tele-gram	kokusai-denpoo
postal money order	yuubin-kawase
postal savings	yuubin-chokin

Post Office

10. Language

Language

1. I'm studying Japanese.

   Watashi-wa nihongo-o benkyoo-shite-imasu.

2. We speak Japanese.

   Watashi-tachi-wa nihongo-o hanashimasu.

3. I can't speak Japanese.

   Watashi-wa nihongo-ga hanasemasen.

4. I can read Japanese, but I can't speak it.

   Nihongo-wa yomemasu-ga hanasemasen.

5. I can read only hiragana.

   Hiragana-nara yomemasu.

6. I can understand Japanese, but I can't speak it.

   Nihongo-o kikitorukoto-wa dekimasu-ga hanasemasen.

7. I don't read many Chinese characters.

   Kanji-wa amari yomemasen.

8. My husband can understand Dutch.

   Shujin-wa orandago-ga wakarimasu.

9. My younger sister

   Imooto-wa

can't understand Vietnamese.

betonamugo-ga wakarimasen.

10. He wants to learn Japanese.

Kare-wa nihongo-o naraitagatte-imasu.

11. My aunt studied Italian.

Oba-wa itariago-o benkyoo-shimashita.

12. That teacher is a Japanese teacher.

Ano-sensee-wa nihongo-no sensee-desu.

Language school

1. I am looking for a good Japanese school.

Ii-nihongo-gakkoo-o sagashite-imasu.

2. Would you please recommend a good Japanese school?

Ii-nihongo-gakkoo-o shookaishite-itadake-masu-ka.

3. I would like to have a personal instructor of Japanese.

Nihongo-no kojinkyooju-ga uketai-no-desu.

4. Do you have a short

Nihongo-no tanki-koosu

course in this school ?	-wa arimasu-ka.
5. What language does the teacher use to teach ?	Jugyoo-wa nani-go-de okonawareru-no-deshoo-ka.
6. What time does the Japanese class start ?	Nihongo-no jugyoo-wa nan-ji-kara-desu-ka.
7. Is the school's library open at night ?	Gakkoo-no toshokan-wa yoru-mo aite-imasu-ka.
8. Can I live in a dormitory ?	Ryoo-ni hairukoto-ga dekimasu-ka.
9. Does this class meet every day ?	Jugyoo-wa mainichi aru-no-desu-ka.
10. When does the summer vacation begin ?	Natsuyasumi-wa itsu-kara-desu-ka.

Miscellaneous

1. Can I pay the lesson fee on the installment plan ?	Jugyoo-ryoo-no bunkatsu-wa dekimasu-ka.

2. Is my pronunciation correct?

Watashi-no hatsuon-wa atte-imasu-ka.

3. Please correct my pronunciation if it's not right.

Hatsuon-ga okashikattara naoshite-kudasai.

4. Would you please interpret for me?

Tsuuyaku-shite-itadakemasu-ka.

INFORMATION

★When you sign a contract, you must pay a deposit and key money and one month advance rent. If you renew your contract, you may have to pay some money to the owner.

Language

Japanese cursive characters	hiragana
the square form of Japanese syllabary	katakana
Chinese characters	kanji
Romanized letters	roomaji
English	Eego
French	Furansugo
German	Doitsugo
Spanish	Supeingo
Italian	Itariago
Portuguese	Porutogarugo
Korean	Kankokugo
Chinese	Chuugokugo
Indonesian	Indonesiago
Thai	Taigo
Arabic	Arabiago
Cantonese	Kantongo
language school	gogaku gakkoo
term	gakki

11. Housing

Looking for a house or apartment

1. Please look for a house for me.

   Heya-o sagashite-itadakemasu-ka.

2. Do you have a suitable house near ∼ ?

   ∼-no chikaku-ni tekitoo-na heya-wa arimasu-ka.

3. I would like to look for a house in the Nakano area.

   Nakano-atari-de sagashitai-no-desu.

4. I would like to find a house along Seibu-Shinjuku line.

   Seebushinjuku-sen ensen-de sagashitai-no-desu.

5. Are there places in which non-Japanese can live?

   Gaikokujin-demo sumeru-tokoro-wa arimasu-ka.

6. Do you have a little larger room?

   Motto hiroi heya-ga arimasu-ka.

7. I don't mind if it's a little smaller room.

   Moochotto semai heya-demo kamaimasen.

8. I'm looking for a

   Koogai-no ikkodate-o

house in the suburbs.   sagashite-imasu.

9. Which floor is it on?   Nan-gai desu-ka.

Equipment

1. Is the room Western [Japanese]-style?   Yooshitsu [Washitsu] desu-ka.

2. Is it furnished?   Kagu-wa tsuite-imasu-ka.

3. Is it a room with tatami mats?   Tatami-no heya desu-ka.

4. How big is the kitchen?   Daidokoro-wa dono-kurai-no hirosa desu-ka.

5. Is there an elevator [a parking lot]?   Erebeetaa [chuushajoo]-wa arimasu-ka.

6. Is it O. K. to install a phone?   Denwa-o tsukete-mo kamaimasen-ka.

7. May I use a gas heater [an oil stove]?   Gasu-sutoobu [Sekiyu-sutoobu]-o tsukatte-moii-desu-ka.

8. Is there a toilet in the room?   Toire-wa heya-ni tsuite-imasu-ka.

9. Is the toilet Western style?   Toire-wa yooshiki desu-ka.

10. I can't use a Japanese style toilet.   Washiki-no toire-wa tsukaemasen.

11. Is there a gas water heater?   Yuwakashiki-wa arimasu-ka.

12. Is there a ventilation system?   Kankisen-wa arimasu-ka.

13. Can I install an air-conditioner?   Eakon-o toritsukete-mo ii-desu-ka.

Neighborhood

1. Is the neighborhood quiet?   Kono atari-wa shizukana tokoro desu-ka.

2. Where is the nearest station?

Ichiban chikai eki-wa doko desu-ka.

3. How far is it from here to the station?

(Koko-kara) Eki-made dono-kurai arimasu-ka.

4. Is there a hospital in the neighborhood?

Chikaku-ni byooin-wa arimasu-ka.

5. Is there a public bath near here?

Chikaku-ni sentoo-wa arimasu-ka.

Rent, etc.

1. How much is the rent?

Yachin-wa ikura desu-ka.

2. I'm looking for a house for less than ¥30,000.

Sanman-en inai-no heya-o sagashite-imasu.

3. I can only go up to ¥50,000.

Goman-en-made dasukoto-ga dekimasu.

4. I don't mind if it's a little more expensive.

Moo sukoshi takakute-mo kamaimasen.

5. What does "key money" mean?

Reekin-wa dooyuu okane desu-ka.

6. How much is the deposit for this house?

Shikikin-wa ikura desu-ka.

7. How much does it come to all together?

Zenbu-de ikura desu-ka.

8. How should I pay every month?

Maitsuki donoyoo-ni shiharaeba ii-desu-ka.

9. How should I pay the bills for electricity, gas, etc.?

Denkidai ya gasudai nado-wa doo sureba ii-deshoo-ka.

Contracts

1. When shall I sign the contract?

Keeyaku-wa itsu desu-ka.

2. Do you need a personal guarantor?

Hoshoonin-wa hitsuyoo-desu-ka.

3. May I write my name instead?

Sain-demo ii-desu-ka.

4. When can I move in? — Itsu-kara hairemasu-ka.

5. How much do I have to pay to renew the contract? — Kooshin-suru-toki-wa ikura haraukoto-ni narimasu-ka.

Miscellaneous

1. What does the owner look like? — Ooyasan-wa donoyoo-na kata-desu-ka.

2. Can I meet the owner? — Ooyasan-ni aisatsusurukoto-ga dekimasu-ka.

3. Please tell me which day of the week I should throw out the garbage [non-burnable]. — Namagomi [Moenai-gomi]-o dasu yoobi-o oshiete-kudasai.

Real estate

realtor, real estate agent	fudoosan'ya
width of two mats (3.3 m²)	hito-tsubo
rent	yachin
deposit	shikikin
rental room with 2-month deposit	shikikin futatsu-no kashishitsu
key money	reekin
apartment with bathroom and toilet	basu-toire-tsuki
apartment with parking	chuushajoo-ari
Children permitted.	Kodomo-ka.
Couples permitted.	Fuufu-ka.
newspaper subscription	shinbundai
water fee	suidoodai
gas fee	gasudai
electric fee	denkidai

NHK (Japan Broadcasting Corporation) fee	jushinryoo
superintendent's fee	kanrihi
general service fee	kyooekihi
house owner	ooyasan
personal guarantor	hoshoonin
caretaker	kanrinin
contract	keeyaku
renewal fee	kooshinryoo

Types of houses

apartment (concrete construction)	manshon
apartment (wood construction)	apaato
wood building	mokuzoo
concrete building	tekkin
∼ dining room and kitchen	∼ DK

～ living room, dining room and kitchen	～ LDK
house	ikkodate
house of ～ stories	～ kai-date
rented house	shakuya
six-mat room	rokujoo
four-and-a-half-mat room	yojoo-han
lodging	geshuku

Interior

entrance	genkan
hall	rooka
closet (Japanese style)	oshiire
floor	furoaa／yuka
display alcove	tokonoma
garden	niwa

Names of rooms

room	heya

living room	ima
children's room	kodomobeya
bedroom	shinshitsu
Japanese-style reception room	zashiki
dining room	shokudoo
kitchen	daidokoro
toilet	toire
toilet	senmenjo
bathroom	furoba
bathroom (with bath-tub)	ofuro
straw mat	tatami
screens of semi-transparent paper	shooji
sliding screen	fusuma
Japanese cushion	zabuton

Real Estate Agent

12. Beauty Parlor, Public Bath

Beauty parlor

1. Give me a perm, please.

   Paama-o kakete-kudasai.

2. I want a soft [tight] permanent, please.

   Yuruku [Kitsuku] paama-shite-kudasai.

3. I'd like just a hair-cut, please.

   Katto-dake onegai-shimasu.

4. I'd like my hair cut just a little, please.

   Honno sukoshi-dake katto-shite-kudasai.

5. I'd like to have my hair cut on the short-side.

   Mijikame-ni kitte-kudasai.

6. Please don't cut it too short.

   Amari mijikaku shinaide kudasai.

7. Make it a little shorter, please.

   Moo sukoshi mijikaku shite-kudasai.

8. Just a trim, please.

   Kesaki-o soroeru-dake-ni shite-kudasai.

9. I'd like my hair a little longer in the

   Ushiro-o sukoshi nagame-ni shite-kudasai.

back.

10. I'd like to have my hair cut to shoulder-length.

Kata-gurai-no nagasa-ni kitte-kudasai.

11. I'd like my ears showing.

Mimi-o dashite-moraemasu-ka.

12. Will I be finished by six ?

Rokuji-made-ni owarimasu-ka.

13. I'd like a set.

Setto-o onegai-shimasu.

14. I want a shampoo and set, please.

Shanpuu-to setto-o shite-kudasai.

15. I want this style, please.

Kono sutairu-ni shite-kudasai.

16. I'd like this style.

Kono katachi-de kekkoo-desu.

17. I'd like a natural look, please.

Shizen-na katachi-ni shiagete-kudasai.

18. I'd like it parted in the middle.

Mannaka-de wake-tai-no-desu.

19. How much will it

Katto-to shanpuu-de

cost to get a haircut   ikura-ni narimasu-ka.
and shampoo?

20. Any beautician is   Dono biyooshi-san-demo
O. K.   kekkoo-desu.

21. Do I need an   Yoyaku-wa hitsuyoo
appointment?   desu-ka.

Barber

1. I want a trim,   Katto-o onegai-shimasu.
please.

2. A shave, please.   Hige-o sotte-kudasai.

3. I'd like my hair   Mae-no kami-wa
short in front, and   mijikaku-shite, ushiro-wa
long in the back.   nagaku-shitai-no-desu.

Public bath

1. Where is the public   Sentoo [Ofuroya]-wa
bath?   doko desu-ka.

2. Is there a public   Kono chikaku-ni sentoo-
bath near here?   wa arimasu-ka.

3. How much is the charge at the public bath?

Sentoo-wa ikura desu-ka.

4. What time does the public bath open?

Sentoo-wa nan-ji-kara desu-ka.

5. Until what time is the public bath open?

Nan-ji-made sentoo-wa aite-imasu-ka.

6. What day of the week is the public bath closed?

Oyasumi-wa itsu desu-ka.

7. Is there a public bath with a coin-operated washing machine?

Koin-randorii-no tsuita ofuroya-wa arimasu-ka.

8. Does the public bath have soap, shampoo, etc?

Sentoo-niwa sekken-ya shanpuu-nado-ga arimasu-ka.

9. May I brush my teeth at the public bath?

Sentoo-de ha-o migaite-mo ii-desu-ka.

10. What should I bring to the bath?   Nani-o motteikeba ii-desu-ka.

11. Is this side the men's [women's] entrance?   Kochira-ga dansee [josee]-no iriguchi desu-ka.

12. Do you have a razor?   Kamisori-wa arimasu-ka.

13. I want to buy a comb.   Kushi-ga kaitai-desu.

14. Should I put my clothes in a locker?   Yoofuku-wa rokkaa-ni ireteoita-hoo-ga ii-desu-ka.

15. I'd like some shampoo and rinse.   Shanpuu-to rinsu-o kudasai.

16. May I use this space?   Koko-o tsukatte-mo ii-desu-ka.

17. Is this shower being used?   Kono shawaa-wa aite-imasu-ka.

18. May I use this faucet?   Kono suidoo-o chotto tsukawasete-kudasai.

19. May I use this basin?

Kono senmenki-o tsukatte-mo ii-desu-ka.

20. May I use a wash cloth in the bathtub?

Yubune-ni taoru-o irete-mo ii-desu-ka.

21. May I put some cold water into the bath?

Mizu-o tashite-mo ii-desu-ka.

22. That bath felt good.

Ii-oyu deshita.

Public Bath

Beauty parlor, barber

beauty parlor	biyooin
barber	tokoya, rihatsuten
cut	katto
shampoo	shanpuu
set	setto
permanent	paama
shave	higesori
sideburns	momiage
mustache	kuchihige
beard	hoohige

Public bath

public bath	sentoo, ofuroya(san)
bathtub	yubune
faucet, tap	karan, jaguchi
basin	senmenki

13. Trouble

Asking for help

1. Help !   Tasukete.

2. What's happened ?   Doo-shita-no-desu-ka.

3. Please   tell   me   Kooban-wa doko-ka
   where the police box   oshiete-kudasai.
   is.

4. Take   me   to   the   Keesatsu-e tsureteitte-
   police, please.   kudasai.

5. Call   the   police, Keesatsu-o yonde-
   please.   kudasai.

6. How can I call the   Koko-kara donoyoo-ni
   police from here ?   keesatsu-o yondara ii-
                          desu-ka.

7. I'd like to notify the Keesatsu-ni
   police.   todokedetai-no-desu.

8. Should I notify the   Keesatsu-ni todoketa-
   police ?   hoo-ga ii-desu-ka.

Lost & Found

1. I lost my ticket.   Kippu-o nakushi-

mashita.

2. I lost my passport near the hotel.

Hoteru-no chikaku-de pasupooto-o otoshi-mashita.

3. My wallet [bicycle] is missing.

Saifu[Jitensha]-ga nakunari-mashita.

4. I left my wallet somewhere.

Saifu-o doko-ka-ni okiwasure-mashita.

5. I forgot my bag on the train.

Densha-no naka-ni kaban-o okiwasure-mashita.

6. I forgot my things in a taxi.

Takushii-ni nimotsu-o wasurete-shimaimashita.

7. I don't remember the car's number.

Kuruma-no bangoo-wa oboete-imasen.

8. I lost my traveler's checks.

Toraberaazu-chekku-o nakushite-shimaimashita.

9. I lost my check.

Kogitte-o funshitsu-shite-shimaimashita.

10. They're American

Amerikan-ekisupuresu-

Express checks.   no-kogitte desu.

11. I got them in Japan.   Nihon-de tsukurimashita.

12. These are the check   Kore-ga kogitte-no
numbers.   bangoo-desu.

13. Can you reissue   Saihakkoo-shite-itadake-
them?   masu-ka.

14. Where should I get   Doko-de saihakkoo-
them reissued?   shite-moraemasu-ka.

15. I'm not sure where I   Doko-ni wasureta-no-ka
left it.   yoku wakarimasen.

16. I lost them yester-   Kinoo nakushimashita.
day.

17. I can't find them   Doko-nimo arimasen.
anywhere.

18. Could you please   Ima sagashite-itadake-
look for it now?   masu-ka.

19. Where is the lost   Ishitsubutsu-
and found?   toriatsukaijo-wa doko-
desu-ka.

20. I have to go to the Thailand Embassy.

Tai-taishikan-ni ikanakereba-narimasen.

21. Would you call me as soon as it's found?

Mitsukari-shidai renraku-shite-moraemasu-ka.

Traffic accidents

1. I had a traffic accident.

Kootsuu-jiko-ni ai-mashita.

2. I had a collision.

Shoototsu-jiko-ni ai-mashita.

3. It's not my fault.

Watashi-ga warui-no-dewa-arimasen.

4. I was within the speed limit.

Seegensokudo-o mamotte-imashita.

5. The traffic light was green.

Shingoo-wa ao deshita.

6. There's an injured person here!

Keganin-ga imasu.

7. Please call an ambulance.

Kyuukyuusha-o yonde-kudasai.

8. My car is stalled.   Kuruma-ga enko-shite-
                          shimaimashita.

9. I have a flat.   Kuruma-ga panku-
                          shimashita.

10. Please help me   Taiya-o torikaeru-no-o
    replace this tire.   tetsudatte-itadakemasu-
                          ka.

Robbery, theft

1. I had my wallet sto-   Saifu-o torare-mashita.
   len.

2. My room was bro-   Doroboo-ni hairare-
   ken into.   mashita.

3. It was just a few   Hon-no suufun-mae-no
   minutes ago.   koto desu.

4. Can I get my bicy-   (Jitensha-wa)
   cle back?   Modottekuru-deshoo-
                          ka.

Missing child

1. I'm lost.

Michi-ni mayoimashita.

2. My child is missing.

Kodomo-ga hagureta-no-desu.

3. My daughter's name is Terri.

Musume-no namae-wa Terii desu.

4. My son is wearing yellow pants.

Musuko-wa kiiroi-zubon-o haite-imasu.

5. My son is five years old.

Musuko-wa gosai desu.

6. Please look for my child.

Kodomo-o sagashite-kudasai.

Emergency Exit

Trouble

police station	keesatsusho
police box	kooban
the lost and found	ishitsubutsu-toriatsukaijo
pickpocket	suri
thief	doroboo
prowler	akisu
fire	kaji
gas leak	gasu-more
parking violation	chuusha-ihan
speeding	supiido-ihan
settling a matter privately	jidan

Insurances

life insurance	seemee-hoken
health insurance	kenkoo-hoken
fire insurance	kasai-hoken
employee's accident compensation insurance	roosai-hoken

14. Illness

Sudden illness

1. Please take me to a hospital.
   Byooin-e tsureteitte-kudasai.

2. Please tell me where the hospital is.
   Byooin-wa doko-ka oshiete-kudasai.

3. I can't move by myself.
   Hitori-dewa ugokemasen.

4. Please help.
   Tasukete-kudasai.

5. Call an ambulance, please.
   Kyuukyuusha-o yonde-kudasai.

6. Call a doctor, please.
   Oishasan-o yonde-kudasai.

Registering at a hospital

1. I'd like to have a medical examination.
   Shinsatsu-ga uketai-no-desu.

2. I don't have an appointment, but it's an emergency.
   Yoyaku-wa arimasen-ga kyuu-o yoo-suru-no-desu.

Describing an illness

1. I feel ill.   Kibun-ga warui-desu.

2. I have a chronic disease.   Jibyoo-ga arimasu.

3. I have a pain in my ～.   ～-ga itai-desu.

4. It hurts here.   Koko-ga itai-desu.

5. There's a sharp pain in my ～.   ～-ga sasu-yoo-ni itamimasu.

6. It's very painful.   Taihen itai-desu.

7. It hurts a little.   Sukoshi itai-desu.

8. I have a terrible cold.   Hidoi-kaze-o hiite-imasu.

9. I have a headache.   Zutsuu-ga shimasu.

10. I feel chilled.   Samuke-ga shimasu.

11. I feel dizzy.   Memai-ga shimasu.

12. I feel nauseous.   Hakike-ga shimasu.

13. I have a fever.   Netsu-ga arimasu.

14. I've got a bit of a fever.   Chotto netsu-ga arimasu.

15. I've got diarrhea.   Geri desu.

16. I have hemorrhoids.   Zi-na-no-desu.

17. I can't explain my   Nihongo-dewa shoojoo-
    condition in Japa-   o setsumee dekimasen.
    nese.

Seeing a doctor

1. Are you going to   Chuusha-o shimasu-ka.
   give me a shot?

2. I'm pregnant.   Ninshin-shite-imasu.

3. I'm allergic to peni-   Penishirin-ni kyozetsu-
   cillin.   hannoo[arerugii]-o
                                okoshimasu.

4. Will I get well   Sugu-ni naorimasu-ka.
   soon?

5. Do I have to stay in   Ansee-ni shite-inakereba-
   bed?   ikemasen-ka.

Often asked questions

1. What's the matter   Doo-shita-no-desu-ka.

with you?

2. What's wrong?	Doko-ka warui-no-desu-ka.
3. You don't look well.	Chooshi-ga waru-soo desu-ne.
4. Does it hurt here?	Koko-ga itai-desu-ka.
5. Yes, it does.	Hai, itai-desu.
6. No, it doesn't.	Iie, itaku-arimasen.
7. Do you have any allergies?	Arerugii-wa arimasu-ka.

A friend's illness

1. My friend is sick.	Yuujin-ga byooki desu.
2. He's lost consciousness.	Ishiki-o ushinatte-imasu.
3. Should I stay with him at the hospital?	Watashi-mo issho-ni byooin-ni ita-hoo-ga ii-desu-ka.

Injury

1. I'm injured.   Kega-o shite-imasu.

2. I've broken my leg.   Ashi-no hone-o
                         orimashita.

3. It's bleeding.   Shukketsu-shite-imasu.

4. I've got a cut on the Ude-ni suri-kizu-o
   arm.   tsukurimashita.

5. I sprained my wrist. Tekubi-o nenza-
                         shimashita.

6. I have been burned.   Yakedo-o shimashita.

7. I fell down the   Kaidan-kara ochi-
   stairs.   mashita.

8. I was in a motor-   Ootobai-no-jiko-ni ai-
   cycle accident.   mashita.

9. How long will it   Kizu-ga kanchi-suru-
   take to heal comp-   made-ni dono kurai
   letely?   kakarimasu-ka.

Medicine

1. May I have a pre-   Shohoosen-o itadake-

scription ?

2. Do you have medicine for ~ ?

3. What do you have for a headache ?

4. When should I take it ?

5. Should I take it before[after] each meal ?

6. How much should I take each time ?

7. How many times per day should I take it ?

8. Is this medicine antibiotic ?

9. Is this medicine for a fever ?

masu-ka.

~ no kusuri-wa arimasu-ka.

Zutsuu-niwa nani-ga kikimasu-ka.

Itsu nomu-no-desu-ka.

Shokuji-no-mae[ato]-ni nomu-no-desu-ka.

Ikkai-ni ikutsu nomu-no-desu-ka.

Ichinichi-ni nan-kai nomu-no-desu-ka.

Sore-wa koosee-busshitsu desu-ka.

Kore-wa genetsuzai desu-ka.

Hospital terms

illness	byooki
injury	kega
doctor	oisha-san
nurse	kangofu-san
patient	kanja
hospital	byooin
doctor's office	iin
internal medicine section	naika
surgery section	geka
pediatrics section	shoonika
ear, nose and throat section	jibi-inkooka
ophthalmic section	ganka
dentistry section	shika
obstetrics and gyn(a)ecology section	san-fujinka
reception	uketsuke
consulting room	shinsatsu-shitsu
operation	shujutsu

anesthesia	masui
dietary cure	shokuji-ryoohoo
being in the hospital	nyuuin
out patient	taiin
emergency	kyuukan
ambulance	kyuukyuusha

Disease names

headache	zutsuu
stomachache	itsuu
toothache	shitsuu
nausea	hakike
chill	samuke
dizziness	memai
cough	seki
inflamation	kabure
burn	yakedo
diarrhea	geri
constipation	benpi
hangover	futsukayoi
insect bite	mushisasare

cold	kaze
pneumonia	haien
tonsilitis	hentoosen'en
appendicitis	moochooen
sprain	nenza
fracture	kossetsu
hives	jinmashin
itch	kayumi

Parts of the body

body	karada
head	atama
face	kao
forehead	hitai
eyebrows	mayuge
eyelashes	matsuge
eye	me
cheek	hoo
ear	mimi
nose	hana
mustache, beard	hige
tooth	ha

mouth	kuchi
lip	kuchibiru
tongue	shita
chin, jaw	ago
throat	nodo
neck	kubi
shoulder	kata
chest	mune
breast(s)	chibusa
stomach and intestines	onaka
back	senaka
waist, hips	koshi
hips, buttocks	oshiri
arm	ude
hand	te
wrist	tekubi
elbow	hiji
toe, finger	yubi
thumb	oyayubi
nail	tsume
foot, leg	ashi

thigh	momo
knee	hiza
calf	fukurahagi
ankle	ashikubi
heel	kakato
sole	tsumasaki
stomach	i
heart	shinzoo
lung	hai
liver	kanzoo
kidney	jinzoo
intestines	choo
womb	shikyuu
bone	hone
blood	chi, ketsueki
blood vessel	kekkan
muscle	kinniku
nerve	shinkee
skin	hifu, hada

Medicines, pills, drugs

medicine	kusuri

90.-03.-01

011 責　　　0.003 №.

014 卸　　★1236

買　1 1⃞　　★1236 現計

3779 №.

pharmacy	kusuriya, yakkyoku
prescription	shohoosen
eye drops	megusuri
stomach medicine	igusuri
headache medicine	zutsuuyaku
cold medicine	kazegusuri
medicine for diarrhea	geridome
ointment to soothe itching skin	kayumidome
vitamin pill	bitaminzai
laxative	gezai
aspirin	asupirin
digestive	shookazai
ointment	nankoo
first-aid kit	kyuukyuu-bako
thermometer	taionkee
compress	shippu
bandage	hootai (bando eido)
Band-Aid	band-eido
sticking plaster	bansookoo
sanitary napkin	seeri-yoo-napukin

About the Author

Michiko Kasahara was born in Tokyo and graduated from Japan Women's University. She studied for two years at Takushoku University in the Japanese Instructor Course. She now teaches Japanese at companies and Japanese school.

Title : DAILY JAPANESE
       Words & Phrases
Author : Michiko Kasahara
Publisher : Goken Co., Ltd.
       7-17 Sarugaku-cho 2-chome
       Chiyoda-ku, Tokyo, Japan
       Tel. 03 (291) 3986

定価 1,200円
(in Japanese Currency)